The Rex Motor Bicycle Club's inaugural run culminated at The Swan's Nest Hotel in Stratford-on-Avon in 1903.

VINTAGE MOTOR CYCLE ALBUM

COMPILED & EDITED by DENNIS HOWARD

An MHB Book
Frederick Warne

CONTENTS

Waders by Dennis Howard 4

Motorcycling milkman by A. B. Demaus 6

Four of the best Drawings by David Ansell. Captions by Bob Currie 16

Switcher's tale 18

Moto Vecchia by Dennis Howard 23

Social workshop by Guy Ashenden 29

Pre-war clubman—his life and times by Norman Sanderson 34

Lightweight sidecar by Dennis Howard 50

Came but never conquered by Dennis Howard 58

Low speed thrills and hilarity by Guy Ashenden 64

Riding an EMC in the 1949 International Six Days Trial by Ed Stott 75

Where are you now? by Dennis Howard 84

EMC road test by Mike Jackson 86

The only rising sun by Bill Firth 92

Index 96

Published by Frederick Warne (Publishers) Ltd
London, England, 1982

Copyright © 1982 Frederick Warne (Publishers) Ltd

ISBN 0 7232 2874 4

Designed by Brian Harris and Mark Slade

Printed by William Clowes (Beccles) Ltd, Beccles and London

FOREWORD

Motorcycling is mainly a young man's pursuit, although in some cases it is taken sufficiently seriously by certain individuals to become a way of life when they are well into middle age or indeed over.

Such people should not be judged critically or treated as subjects of derision by the non-motorcycling public. The *mature* motorcyclist is usually representative of a highly interesting minority 'group' classified as *in depth characters*.

The contributors to this Album are all very individualistic beings, some still regularly motorcycling, while others now fully retired from active recreation reflect on their early days when that crude, *it always will be*, but oh! so endearing device, the motorcycle, played so great a part in their personal lifestyle.

Anyone with a touch of the right spirit about him who has not sampled the delights of riding a well set up motorcycle has certainly missed out on one of the most exhilarating, mobile experiences of the twentieth century.

It is hoped that the content of this book will be attractive not only to those immediately identifying with their own motorcycling activities some years ago, but to a younger, current generation who are usually most anxious to learn how the wheels turned in an earlier period.

Dennis Howard pictured on Guy Ashenden's Henley Blackburne at Mallory Park a few years ago

ABOUT THE COMPILER

Dennis Howard, the compiler of this book, first legally rode a motorcycle in the early months of 1937 although rides had been indulged in some years before that in England's once quiet country lanes.

His fascination for motorcycles came upon him in what he considers now must have been a gradual process, but his initial moment of indoctrination came on suddenly becoming aware that the local newsagent's model KSS 350cc Velocette was an exciting creation to behold, either at rest or when being stylishly ridden by its owner.

Totally seduced by motorcycles, Dennis Howard set about obtaining his own machine, the first of a long line of second-hand models being a strange combination of a 250cc Villiers two-stroke engine fitted into a Rudge frame of most doubtful parentage. Perhaps his favourite pre-war mount however was an HRD Python, being yet again an assembly job, but professionally built, where a 500cc Rudge Ulster engine powered along the cycle parts of an HRD (later Vincent). This machine exuded sportiness as Howard recalls, with its huge black Brooklands 'can' that stood way out past the HRD's rear wheel and secured with the customary drilled bracket.

After service with H.M. Forces, Dennis Howard joined the editorial staff of *The Motor Cycle* and today marvels at the fact that a genuine stitched back journal was produced weekly, where today such a thing is only possible with a 'monthly', if that.

Of his years with Iliffes he recalls them as near sacred with so much going on in the immediate post-war motorcycle world of a truly exciting nature. Here road racing, being his favourite branch of motorcycle sport, was still referred to as *classic* even by the BBC whose radio commentaries were of great quality.

Leaving *The Motor Cycle* in the early 1950s, Dennis Howard set out on his special freelance motorcycling way of life which embraced competition work, motorcycle manufacture and sales, writing about them, and with the odd race meeting commentary made from time to time.

Howard's current thoughts on the motorcycle scene are perhaps surprising in that he considers that the sport is in danger of being overplayed and that the grossness of so many road machines will eventually push the legislators into imposing certain unpleasant restrictions on motorcycling generally. In order that there should exist a healthy future, Dennis Howard suggests that much more emphasis should be placed on motorcycles serving the purpose for which they were originally intended, to provide economical road transport. This need not be dull in any way he says, and he speaks with much authority on the subject, being an everyday motorcyclist.

WADERS

In which we mourn the passing of those good, old-fashioned waders. Anyone who remembers hitching up his Hutchinson's will share in the nostalgia, and for those who do not, let DENNIS HOWARD recall their halcyon days.

Long gone from the motorcycling scene are motorcycling waders—not that these excellent items were ever quite intelligent enough to take a ride without assistance, as my opening line might suggest, but in order to differentiate between waders manufactured for other purposes—fishing, for example—reference to waders 'motorcycling for the use of' will give the right impression.

Quite a bit different in design and to a degree construction were motorcycling waders from any other thigh-length jobs where absolute waterproofing qualities were required. Made of rubber with a stockinet lining, they were purpose-built on the large size in order that the wearer could step straight into them, shoes and all. Being thigh length, as I have mentioned, one could wear one's best trousers if necessary and be assured that at the end of the filthiest journey one remained totally clean and, perhaps even more to the point, dry.

On the exterior, waders on the foot end were substantial with a long moulded sole, including the very mildest of heels. On the uppers, their shape represented more or less a foot, with a securing strap over the instep to prevent any possibility of the wearer's foot inadvertently working its way up the leg part. There existed more sophisticated versions that had special

reinforcements in the way of moulded patches, particularly for one's kick-starter leg and whose duty it was to prevent any serious chafing of the rubber when the kickstart was operated.

In dry conditions waders were either contained in a special wader bag or just folded as neatly as it was possible to do with such things, and secured to the top of one's petrol tank, but always at the ready if required.

The best names in the manufacture of motorcycling waders were Hutchinson, Dunlop and the Gutta-Percha company, but rather as all vacuum cleaners, regardless of individual manufacturers, are more than often referred to as Hoovers, the motorcyclist got into the habit of talking about his Hutchinson waders even if he were stepping out into all the dirty stuff of an unpleasant day in Dunlop or Gutta-Percha's best.

One might question how motorcycling waders were secured to their wearer's waist in order to prevent them falling down. This was simplicity itself for each wader was quite individual to a leg, each having a securing strap that

fastened the topmost part of the wader to the wearer's braces or trousers belt as the case may have been.

Sometimes the charactered, hard riding motorcyclist was seen to have numerous inner tube repair patches dotted about his wader, sealing off yet another leaky area in a well-worn set of these items. However, there came a time when these patches became rather offensive to the eye and sufficiently pointed remarks even from one's best friend more than persuaded the wearer to nip down to Marble Arch Motor Supplies for a new pair of ordinaries at nine shillings and sixpence, or best quality Hutchinsons at eighteen bob.

The sensible wader went out of fashion, alas, in the early 1950s, to be replaced by footwear that was—and indeed remains—totally unsuitable for serious wet weather riding over long distances. Rubber Wellington boots have certain limitations in that they do not permit one to wear one's walking shoes beneath, while even the best leather motorcycling boots will never remain totally waterproof for long. On the other hand [rather, foot],

waders have everything in their favour and should be reintroduced, although they no longer need to be dreary black but produced in a variety of colours in a modern way.

Only a few years ago I wrote to Dunlops suggesting that the company should seriously consider manufacturing motorcycling waders once again. Although in his letter of acknowledgement the manager of the appropriate department confessed that he was not quite sure exactly what motorcycling waders were, he assured me that whatever they were there was no demand for such things! Well, if there might exist the nicest possible tendency to cast aside that longing for 'image' motorcycling footwear and call for something really sensible like motorcycling waders, who knows? Dunlops could be in business along this line. Vintage, post-vintage and post-war enthusiasts take note!

The suggested kit for 1945 riding may appear distinctly old fashioned for the motorcyclist of the 1980s. However, the pair of waders shown on the left, being just perfect for long distance work in wet weather, and very warm too, hath no equal in the most favourable way.

MOTORCYCLING MILKMAN

Motorcycle competition in the days before the Great War is seldom chronicled nowadays, which makes A. B. Demaus's interesting account of Ray Abbott's career as a wholesale dairyman and talented rider all the more appealing, especially with such a fine collection of early photographs to accompany it.

A. B. Demaus was first 'introduced' to a motorcycle at the tender age of four when placed on the pillion of a family friend's machine sometime in 1917. Later the writer speaks of being frightened out of his wits by a horde of trials riders storming a steep, rough and overgrown footpath while climbing a hillside in the Chilterns. However, by the time the first half dozen had passed, Mr Demaus had decided that the noise, speed and general atmosphere were quite thrilling and so took every opportunity to be in the vicinity at weekends when such things were happening. Once, the young Demaus got into dire trouble when caught

on the pillion of a motorcycle belonging to a 'singularly sporting but somewhat non-academic schoolmaster' who gave flat-out circuits round the cricket pitch by way of special rewards to deserving pupils. The master eventually got the sack and A. B. Demaus received six of the best.

Now a schoolmaster himself, Mr Demaus suggests that this may or may not account for an interest in motorcycles being more academic than practical, having owned only two vintage machines before passing to four wheels, 'still vintage', adds ABD.

He has written innumerable articles

and several books on motoring, motorcycling and cycling topics, particularly in a period 'of the palmy days before 1939', being, as the modern expression goes, A. B. Demaus's scene.

'Mr Abbott stands over 6ft high and rides 13 stone; a burly giant indeed. He is a native of London, a wholesale dairyman by trade . . . a typical Saxon in appearance, ruddy complexion, fair moustache, a fine specimen of British manhood . . . (and) has been known

Shaw and Drake, two P & M riders in the 1912 Six Days, returning to Taunton, HQ of the event, after one of the day's runs.

Mrs Hardee [3½ P & M], one of the brave lady competitors in the same event, draws an admiring crowd.

The ladies again: Mrs Hardee [3½ P & M] and Miss Hammett [2¾ Douglas] returning through Taunton after one of the runs in 1912.

J. R. Haswell [Triumph] was rewarded with second place in the Senior TT, 1912, being the first private owner to finish and the first single cylinder machine—this at a time when the pros and cons of singles *versus* twins were being hotly debated. Winner, however, was a twin, F. A. Applebee, seen here on the left astride his Scott.

for some years as a daring motorcyclist competing in many reliability trials . . .' Behind this rather dated prose lies both understatement of what had been and, not unnaturally, lack of knowledge of what was yet to come. Those words were written in June 1913 when Ray Abbott had come home in second place in the Senior TT on his Rudge, a mere 5 seconds behind winner Tim Wood on a Scott. Even at that date, as the contemporary reporter hinted, Ray Abbott was a motorcyclist of wide and varied experience. After the war he was to extend his motor competition activities to four wheels, a very successful two-wheel career behind him.

It has recently been my good fortune to come into possession of a large quantity of Abbott's personal photographs and mementoes which have provided a fascinating insight into his motoring activities, though I would certainly not claim that what follows is by any means exhaustive. By 1913, the year of his greatest success on 'The Island', he was already an old hand, having competed not only in the TTs of 1910 and 1912, but in the major trials, including the Six Days, and at Brooklands on many occasions. There, in August 1909, in the August Motorcycle Handicap, he came 2nd 'from 45 seconds' in the First Roadster Handicap on his 3½hp Triumph, behind Lee-Evans (Indian) whose winning speed was 60·5 mph. In the second similar handicap event of the meeting he was, alas, unplaced, though Lee-Evans pulled off another win with his Indian at 57·5 mph. In the Junior Motorcycle Handicap Abbott could not better fifth place, the race being won by L. C. Munro (NSU) at 50 mph.

1910 found Abbott competing in the series of ACU Quarterly Trials, the first of which was run off early in the year in usually foul weather conditions. His mount was a big 8hp Matchless combination. Heavy rain had fallen the previous day and a hard frost during the night turned the roads into sheets of ice and made the conditions treacherous in the extreme. Dashwood Hill—the old Dashwood, that is, and not its modern and almost unnoticed counterpart on the A40, now itself superseded by the M40—out of West Wycombe caused the literal downfall

The magic of 'The Island': Haswell [Triumph] overtakes Jones [Rudge] while descending Bray Hill at 70 mph during the Senior TT in 1912.

Almost certainly taken on Kop Hill near Princes Risborough, a speeding motorcyclist heads up the hill while the smoke from the starting cannon disperses and the operating marshal looks stunned by the reverberations!

MCC 4th Winter Club Run. Two solo riders on a Douglas and an NUT respectively, start from the Bridge House Hotel, Staines, on this classic Christmas event.

MCC Jarrott Cup Trial, 22nd March 1913. J. Dawson [Clyno combination] seen at the start, again at Staines Bridge, in the wee sma' hours of a dark wet morning.

of many of the solo entries, a commentator remarking that at any one time many riders and machines could be seen off the road altogether or lying prone with their machines on top of them, thus baulking other competitors as the ice-rink conditions prevented them scrambling rapidly out of the way. *The Motor Cycle* remarked that Abbott climbed Dashwood in excellent form, but most of the other passenger machines were in trouble with varying degrees of back-wheel slip. Abbott was one of but few riders who obtained full marks on this hill. Apart from the hazards of route and weather that faced all competitors in the event equally, Abbott's only problem during the trial was the breakage of a belt fastener. This very tough event, which was the precursor of the other Quarterly Trials in the series throughout the year, attracted 74 entrants. Of Abbott's performance in this event, *Motor Cycling*'s reporter commented: 'The Matchless sidecar went splendidly and as I rode behind it for a long way I can testify as to the excellent running of this combination'.

The great highlight of the sporting calendar was, of course, the TT, for which event Abbott was on the Isle of Man in late May, busy practising with his 3½hp Rex 'Speed King'. As a mark of respect to King Edward VII, who was laid to rest on the Friday preceding the race, no practice periods were permitted on that day. Comment was made that Abbott was very fast round the corners and that 'apart from the scrap metal strewing the highway, the surface of the road is much better than last year'. There were 83 entries for the great event that year, Abbott's Rex being one of no fewer than 17 of this make, made up of five works entries, ridden by O. C. Godfrey, A. H. Alexander, F. A. Applebee, A. J. Sproston and R. Lord, and twelve independent entries of which eleven were private owners, as was Abbott, of course. The Rex works team had their headquarters at the Ballacraine Hotel.

The Snaefell Hill Climb formed part of the general attractions of TT week, and in this event Abbott's Rex came 17th out of 18 entries in his class for single cylinder machines not exceeding 500cc that had competed in the TT itself. Among the noteworthy entries

in this class were W. G. McMinnies (3½ Triumph), who was 7th, F. W. Barnes (3½ Zenith-Gradua) 8th, 'Pa' Norton (3½ Norton) 14th and F. W. Applebee (3½ Centaur), who trailed Abbott into 18th place in the class. Fastest time of the day was made by 3½ Triumph mounted W. F. Newsome.

The next major event in Abbott's calendar for 1910 was the Six Days which that year took the form of an 'end-to-end' run from Land's End to John O'Groats. In giving his impressions of the event, the Rev. B. H. Davies (*Ixion* of *The Motor Cycle*) remarked on the fact that by comparison with the 1908 and 1909 events, that of 1910 was 'a severe route with regulations twice as severe as any previous trial'. Although the inclusion of Amulree was much criticized by many as being a 'freak' hill, unsuitable for inclusion in the event, *Ixion* justified its inclusion on the grounds that such a demanding hill encouraged the more widespread use of variable gears. Abbott rode a big 8hp Matchless combination in this event of 1,019 very tough miles. Although he had to shed his passenger momentarily on Amulree, his climb of this hill attracted favourable comment. Alas, he had to retire on the penultimate day of the event through persistent tyre trouble, having run 30 miles with a cover stuffed with grass.

In the autumn of 1910 Abbott competed in the final round of the ACU Quarterly Trials with the 8hp Matchless combination again, but immediately previous to that event he was in action at Brooklands on Saturday, 8th October, at the 'Bemsee' 100-Mile High Speed Reliability Trials, an event that attracted an entry of over 60 machines. An unscheduled excitement here was a determined effort at Sutteism by E. W. Scofield's motorcycle, appropriately named *Red Terror*. This machine, which *Motor Cycling* described as 'an ancient Humber', caught fire in a big way, and it was Abbott who raced up the track and obtained a fire extinguisher—one of those large conical devices akin to a witch's hat—with which to put out the blaze. *Motor Cycling* portrayed him using it to good effect while a ring of spectators stood by in apparently passive amazement.

For the 1912 Six Days, the ACU's headquarters were situated at Clarke's Hotel, Taunton, which formed the centre for the 10th Annual Six Days Reliability Trial. In this event competitors were sent out daily to cover

W. E. Cook [3½ ASL] passes P. Butler [3½ Scott] in the early stages of the 1913 Senior race.

R. Holloway corners his 3½hp Premier at the Ramsey hairpin during the early stages of the 1913 Senior. Two or three of the small children seem blasé or just preoccupied!

Billy Heaton takes his AJS round Bray Corner in the 1913 Junior event. The AJS triumph was to come the following year.

distances ranging from 150½ miles to 196½ miles, returning each night to Taunton. The routes took in the majority of the West Country's most notorious hills, some of which featured on more than one day of the Trial. Porlock and Lynmouth, Countisbury and Barbook Mill featured on the second day, Birdlip on the third and, for good measure, Porlock and Lynmouth again on the last day, the total mileage for the event being 1,000. As well as such notorious gradients, much of the route contained other stiff, but lesser hazards.

Abbott rode his 3½hp Bradbury with NSU gear in this event, and among the 131 entrants listed in the programme (which even contained gradient profiles for each day's run) there were many well-known names, among them Jesse Baker (Scott), W. H. Bashall (BAT), George Brough (Brough), H. Greaves (Enfield), W. G. McMinnies (Triumph—one of the very few single gear machines competing), H. F. S. Morgan (Morgan) and A. J. Stevens (AJS). Two ladies bravely tested both their own stamina and that of their machines in this gruelling event, these being Miss R. Hammett, who rode a 2¾hp Douglas and Mrs Mabel Hardee mounted on a 3½hp P & M. As for the other entries, the variety was almost infinite, ranging from the well-known and established marques to representatives of makes seldom heard of, whose names have long since sunk into oblivion.

The early days of September of that year brought another noteworthy Abbott performance when Ray invited a small party of North London enthusiasts to accompany him to Henley to tackle the dreaded Arms Hill (more frequently rendered as 'Alms Hill' in later years). Here, in ideal weather conditions but with the surface of the hill described as treacherous, he attempted to take his single cylinder Bradbury with wickerwork bodied sidecar, and passenger up the hill. At his first attempt, despite having roped the rear wheel, the machine lost its grip of the surface and came to a halt. On the second attempt, however, Abbott picked a careful route, hugging the hedge, and the machine climbed unhesitatingly to the top with its 21 stone human load. For good measure another run was made, H. E. P. Parker now riding in place of Abbott. This, too, was successful. Needless to say, Bradbury's made much of this success,

F. Applebee [3½ Scott], who retired after completing two laps in the Senior race of 1913. Victory went to Tim Wood on another Scott, however.

F. R. Bateman was a tragic victim of the 1913 Senior event, crashing his Rudge at Keppel Gate and later dying from his injuries. Here he is portrayed a few weeks earlier at Brooklands. Leaning over his shoulder is F. Clarke, Foreman Tester at Rudge-Whitworth Ltd.

the first climb of the hill by a single cylinder machine, in their advertisements, stressing that the model was a standard 3½hp Bradbury, chain driven and with a two speed gear. Abbott himself kept for posterity a 'certificate' signed by a number of witnesses testifying as to the validity of the climb. This was written on a sheet of notepaper headed 'The Bull Hotel, Henley-on-Thames'.

The year 1912 also brought him a Gold Medal and a special prize in the Essex MC's 24-hour London-York-London Trial in which he competed with a Bradbury sidecar combination in the passenger class. But for Abbott, 1913 was to be a year of even greater successes, of which no doubt the sweetest was in that peer of motorcycle events, the Tourist Trophy. Earlier in the year, in the latter days of March, the MCC held their London-Land's End-London Trial for the Jarrott Cup, an event which brought a record entry list of 110, of whom 95 turned out for the start, the first of them W. E. S. May (8hp Matchless) and the indefatigable Rear-Admiral Sir R. K. Arbuthnot (3½hp Triumph) being flagged away from Staines Bridge at the grisly hour of 3.00a.m. Abbott was again Bradbury mounted and started with his old friend and rival H. E. Parker, of whom we last heard as a fellow contestant with Abbott in the successful climb of Arms Hill, Henley, the previous year. As *The Motor Cycle* remarked, 'Bad weather dogged the Trial throughout the outward journey and was the cause of considerable discomfort . . .' but this relented later, allowing the 55 competitors who had qualified for the return trip to have a pleasant and largely uneventful homeward run. But, as always, thoughts were increasingly focused on the island as Spring turned to Summer, and the last week of May 1913 found the Isle of Man a swarm of activity.

Abbott suffered a minor spill at Keppel Gate in practice and was then told that he, in company with the other Rudge riders, was too noisy! One wonders if this referred to the men or their machines! Rudges were well represented, there being no fewer than 12 of the make in the Senior event. *Motor Cycling* remarked that it was a great struggle to get up at 4.00a.m., but despite the fact that it was raining there was quite a fair sized crowd of spectators at Quarter Bridge. Abbott

As soon as the TT excitement died down, Abbott was one of a record entry from 41 clubs for the MCC Inter-Team Trials, based on Chipping Norton, Oxon, where many of the competitors are seen here assembled.

went past that spot at 4.45a.m. in company with fellow Rudge rider Kremleff, a Russian.

Race day itself dawned sunny and hot, scorchingly so as the forenoon wore on, and the Senior race was not due to start until 12.30p.m. Over 100 riders waited in the heat under starter's orders, first man away being, by tradition, the previous year's winner, in this case, F. A. Applebee (3½ Scott). By the end of the first lap, four Rudges (but not Abbott's) and two Indians were in the leading positions and already it was apparent that speeds in this Senior event were going to be higher than ever before. By the end of the second lap, Sheard's leading position with his Rudge was being challenged by Tim Wood (Scott), the eventual winner. Abbott had pushed into 6th position, which caused *Motor Cycling's* reporter to comment, 'Till this TT Abbott has not shone with any particular brilliance at speed work, but is now riding as well as anyone'. He was also commended for his cornering

ability, the same reporter crediting him with 'the best bit of cornerwork that had been shown up to that time'. By the end of the first day's racing Tim Wood (Scott) was in the lead in the Senior; Abbott finished the first day in fifth position. After an intervening day the race was resumed on the Friday, both Junior and Senior contestants racing together. The machines having been under guard in the meanwhile could not be worked on at all, thus at 9.00a.m. on the Friday morning, when they were wheeled out to resume the battle for the Trophy, some faltering starts and mechanical bothers were not unexpected. Bateman, a Rudge works team rider and a man of great promise, unfortunately crashed at Keppel Gate and died later from his injuries. The day was a good deal cooler than it had been on the previous race day and again speeds were high. Mechanical bothers and 'running out of road' were prevalent, too. In a tense and exciting finish, Tim Wood's Scott, which actually completed the last lap after Abbott had already done so, won by 5 seconds since he had time in hand from his first day's lead over Abbott.

Interviewed after the race, Abbott said the race was 'a glorious blind' and

'Never enjoyed anything so much in my life'. He had had no mechanical trouble whatsoever, had never used the exhaust-lifter but had controlled the machine solely on the multi-gear and the throttle, and his only stops had been to fit a new belt and sparking plug. He was also the first private competitor to finish.

Abbott's lap times were:

Lap 1	47m 34s
Lap 2	45m 49s
Lap 3	46m 21s
Lap 4	45m 55s
Lap 5	46m 34s
Lap 6	48m 21s
Lap 7	45m 49s
TOTAL	5h 26m 23s

and an overall speed of 48·27 mph.

Following almost immediately that successful TT came the MCC's Tenth Anniversary Team Trial, which that year was centred on Chipping Norton, Oxfordshire, with the event HQ at The White Hart Hotel. Abbott, with his 3½ Bradbury, rode as a member of the Walthamstow MCC and was No. 366 of this large field of 41 teams from clubs up and down the country.

July found him competing in the French Grand Prix with his Rudge in

Another 1913 Senior contestant was H. Petty [Singer], who is seen here with this machine at Brooklands shortly prior to the TT.

A general view of the start of the North Middlesex MCC Open Trial as competitors meet at the Old Gatehouse, Highgate.

Abbott's Triumph entry in the 1914 Senior brought him no luck. He is seen here rounding the famous Ramsey hairpin.

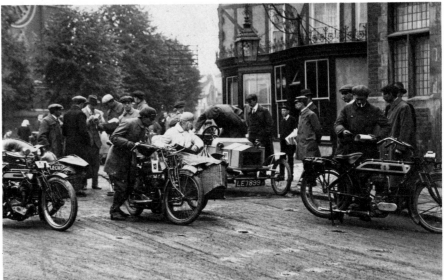

the 500cc class, but despite the fact that he managed to record the fastest speed over a measured kilometre (61·79 mph) the machine was not on form. With the bike running somewhat irregularly he could only manage 7th place in the 500cc class with an overall time of 4h 59m 4s.

Three weeks later it was Abbott's turn to act as one of the hosts to an invited team of Dutch motorcyclists in the English-Dutch 'International' Trial which started from Oxford and was held on 4th August 1913. The route had been kept secret until the morning of the event and when revealed it consisted of what Rudge-Whitworth Ltd, in their booklet for the year, described as 'many steep declivities with indifferent surfaces', going on to cite such as Nap Hill, Kop Hill, High Wycombe's Station Hill and Beacon Hill, among others. Subsequently, the two teams and senior officials travelled to Coventry where, at the invitation of Rudge-Whitworth Ltd, they were entertained to luncheon, followed by a tour of the Rudge works. The overall result of this 'international' trial was a handsome win for the British team.

In May of 1914 Abbott temporarily deserted two wheels (or three) for four, driving one of a team of three Deemster light cars in the Light Car Trial, a strenuous event of over 1,000 miles. In Class C (cars not exceeding 200 guineas in price) there were a number of makes represented, including Singer, Standard, Hillman, AC, Sirron and Charronnette. The Deemsters were out of luck, Abbott retiring on the first day of the Trial, one non-starting, and the other also retiring on the first day. Nevertheless, a portent of things to come, maybe?

Later in that ominous year, 1914, Abbott again rode in the Senior TT, this time mounted on a 3½hp Triumph, but the good fortune of the previous year deserted him and he was never up with the leaders. Indeed, a reporter commented 'Ray Abbott (Triumph) was not putting up the show he did last year', although he and Jack Woodhouse (3½ Quadrant) had a great duel among the back markers on the first lap. To rub salt in the wound, so to speak, it was a Rudge that C. G. Pullin rode to victory in that year's Senior.

Late in June 1914 Abbott was much busied with the Essex MC's event at Southend, held in splendid weather on the Western Esplanade. The event attracted a big entry list and a crowd of some 15,000 spectators. Abbott's role in this popular event was not this time as a competitor but as Assistant Starter. He and his 'chief', Mr W. Cooper, must have been kept amply busy dealing with the 226 'motorbikes' and 82 cars that comprised the entry list, according to a local newspaper. However, one can safely assume that this somewhat inflated figure was arrived at by adding all the entries for the various classes which, in fact, would have been repetitive in many cases. Indeed, that paper's own results confirm this.

All too soon, Abbott, like so many thousands of others, was in uniform fighting in France, and when peace returned and motoring came back into its own again, Abbott turned to four-wheeled competition in which he was to gain an impressive list of successes, but these have no part in a work concerned with motorbikes!

THE MATCHLESS G80CS, 1953.

FOUR OF THE BEST

Drawings by David Ansell, a twenty-six year old former architect, now a free lance illustrator, browser and researcher, specializing in the early post-war period of the British motorcycle industry.

Mr Ansell, who is acknowledged as one of this country's leading illustrators for various motorcycle publications, owns a small stable of Matchless and AJS machines plus, as he says, 'the odd Panther or two'.

Essay captions by Bob Currie, over twenty-one and a dedicated motorcyclist for most of his life. Mr Currie correctly mourns the passing of large scale manufacture of British bikes, particularly in his native Birmingham.

An expert in motorcycle recognition, few would wish to challenge his unique ability to get things right first time, whether a question or faded old photograph is presented to him. Possessing a vast storehouse of motorcycle knowledge, Triumph riding Bob Currie is ideally suited to hold the post of Midlands editor of the newspaper *Motor Cycle Weekly*, formerly *The Motor Cycle*. More recently he has been appointed editor of *The Classic Motor Cycle*.

Far cry from the screaming Japanese motocrossers of today it may be, yet the Matchless G80CS was a pretty formidable competitor in

the big scrambles of the mid to late 1950s, particularly when handled by an expert like the late and much missed Brian Stonebridge.

It was Stonebridge, in fact, who scored a resounding win in the 500cc class of the Sunbeam Point-to-Point of 1953 on a model almost like the one featured here—almost, but not quite, because the registration plates would have been removed on the race occasion. Based on the roadgoing 498cc model G80, this one was the CS or 'Competition Springer'. There was also the G80C, being a rigid-frame version for the trials man ... because it was thought at the time that unless the rear end was 'solid' there would be loss of traction in observed sections of a trial's course. The wheelbase was shorter than the road job, plus a higher ground clearance.

Other departures from standard embraced a small light-alloy fuel tank [note the short pillars raising it from the mounting brackets], a close ratio gearbox, Lucas 'Wader' magneto with manual ignition control and, most important of all, a light alloy cylinder head.

In due course there would be other star Matchie men, such as Dave Curtis and world champion Rene Baeten of Belgium, although it has to be admitted that for most of the time the G80CS had to play second fiddle to its big rival from Birmingham, the BSA Gold Star. However, with the optional extra lighting set

supplied and fitted and registration plates firmly secured in place, the Matchless made an ideal explorer's special.

Canny as they come, old Joah Phelon had patented the idea of using an engine in place of the frame front down tube of bicycle type machines as long ago as 1900 and it was still a distinguishing feature of the 'big sloper' when the last Panther motorcycle left the Cleckheaton factory. No P & M [Phelon & Moore] motorcycle was ever belt driven. At first a side valve of 500cc, it was chosen by the Royal Flying Corps as their standard machine in the Great War and it stayed on to do service with the fledgling RAF. Redesigned to overhead valve configuration by Granville Bradshaw of ABC fame in 1923, the name 'Panther' was then applied for the first time.

Two works Panthers were entered for the 1924 Senior TT and were equipped with such novelties for the period as four-speed gearboxes and internal expanding brakes on each wheel. It seems a pity that on this, the marque's TT début, neither bike finished because their respective riders had collided with each other.

The 598cc sloper was introduced in 1927 although it did not gain its Model 100 classification until some three years later. Other Panthers came and went—a 250cc transverse vee-twin, Villiers engined two strokes, the Red Panthers of the despairing 1930s, while the Big Pussy soldiered on, usually hauling a vast saloon sidecar full of Mum and the children. There was a 650cc edition, the Model 120, which fans called the Biggest Aspidistra in the World—and all in one pot. By 1964, however, the Panther was at last put down. There was no option, for Burman gearboxes were no longer made as separate items [unit construction being the 'in thing'] and the Lucas Magdyno was out of production. Somehow a unit construction Big Pussy with alternator electrics would not have been the same.

© DAVID ANSELL

THE PANTHER MODEL 100
SPRING FRAME, DE LUXE, 1957.

© DAVID ANSELL

THE ARIEL MODEL 4G,
SQUARE FOUR, 1956.

© DAVID ANSELL

THE A.J.S. MODEL 20,
1951.

Legend has it that one-time ship's wireless operator Edward Turner travelled up from London to Birmingham with the idea of a four cylinder engine in which the cylinders would be arranged two-by-two, scribbled on the back of a cigarette packet. It is said that Turner hawked the scheme all round the Midlands industry until, at last, Ariel boss Jack Sangster decided to give him a chance. The result was the Square Four, a 500cc with chain-driven overhead camshaft, sensation of the 1930 Motorcycle Show at Olympia. A 600cc version followed a couple of years later, but enthusiasts found that the cammy Squariel, however pleasantly smooth to ride, suffered from inadequate cooling of the cylinder head. The only real answer was a complete revamp, this being undertaken for the 1937 programme with the Square Four emerging as a push-rod ohv model of 600 and later 1000cc.

It had a different bottom-end assembly with the two crankshafts geared on the nearside instead of in the middle. The engine unit remained of cast iron, however, and the 1939 addition of the special compensated-link plunger rear suspension added yet more weight to an already portly machine. So did the telescopic front forks adopted for the post-war return of the model to the Ariel range. Again the answer was a revamp and by throwing away the cast iron cylinder block and head and substituting light alloy, 33lb were saved. There was to be one more major change in 1954 when the Square Four reached its peak with the four-pipe Mark II Model 4G, the most gentlemanly multi of them all.

There could have been yet another version with swinging arm rear suspension, but it was not to be. Ariels were committed to the Leader two stroke twin, and four strokes, the Square Four among them, were given the old heave-ho.

In one very important respect, the 498cc Model 20 AJS [and its Matchless counterpart, of course] differed from every other post-war British vertical twin. Its crankshaft was carried on *three* main bearings—two outer roller races, and a plain bearing carried on a plate clamped between the two crankcase halves. Other details included independent barrels very deeply spigoted into the crankcase mouth, and independent cylinder heads. Rather ingeniously, grooves cut around the outside of each cylinder barrel skirt served as integral features of the rocker box and camshaft oil feed systems.

The idea of the centre bearing, of course, was to make the crankshaft assembly as rigid as possible, thereby [it was hoped] reducing engine vibration to a minimum. Alas, it did no such thing, and the Ajay and Matchie twins soon gained an unenviable reputation of shaking the rider's teeth loose at anything above 65 mph. Foul calumny!...well, perhaps ...but they did start with the big disadvantage of having been built south of Watford, thus causing them to be objects of suspicion [if not derision] to any right thinking Midlander. Then there was that funny rear suspension business. AMC, who built the Model 20 in their Woolwich plant, eschewed proprietary rear damper units and, instead, fitted fat dampers of their own design. The fans termed these 'jampots' and the name stuck.

The first models introduced in 1949 were reserved for export, but home supplies began a year later. A fatter bore [72mm, as against 66mm], while retaining the same 72.8mm stroke, produced the companion 592cc Model 30 of the later 1950s. Later came 646cc, and finally 745cc AJS twins, but by then Woolwich was coming apart at the seams and the bigger alleged Ajay was really a Norton.

SWITCHER'S TALE

For those who do not know what a switcher is, read on! This is the tale of MARGARET NYLANDER, a pioneer lady motorcyclist in Australia with an entertaining story to tell.

Melbourne, Australia, 1916, and in Sydney Road, Brunswick, stood the Empire Theatre, a regular picture palace in the new way of things and showing two full-length films nightly. Some distance away in another part of town is another theatre providing the same entertainment. Now when the folks in the Empire had seen their first film and the lights went up, it was quickly put back into the can and rushed to the other theatre by a motorcyclist, whose duty it then was to pick up the film just shown there, returning to the Empire with it where it would be shown in the second half. In other words, two films serving two theatres all in the one night, the success

of the whole operation depending to a considerable degree on the motorcyclist (the Switcher) doing the high speed act of exchange across town.

The Switcher at this time was Dave Brewster, quite an ace as a local motorcycle racer, and later to put up some very good performances in the Isle of Man TT races. It was thirsty work being a Switcher, and it just so happened that bang next door to the Empire Theatre was a nice little confectionery shop, serving all kinds of refreshing drinks, owned and run by Margaret Nylander, a very attractive twenty-three year old.

After downing a bottle of suitably refreshing liquid one evening, Brews-

ter told Miss Nylander that he wanted to ride in a race meeting at Geelong Road, Melbourne, very soon although this would conflict with his film switching job ... what could he do? Well again it just so happened that Miss Nylander had owned a 225cc Baby Triumph, the little paddle-start two stroke with a two speed gearbox, and had been taught to ride it by one of the electricians at the Empire. So the girl could ride a bike and knew all about it. Indeed she had run her latest job, a 7hp Indian Powerplus model in solo

So the girl can use a bike and knows all about it! Miss N's first machine, the Baby Triumph on which she learned to ride.

'Even finding time to drive the little Model T Ford fitted out as a Red Cross ambulance'.

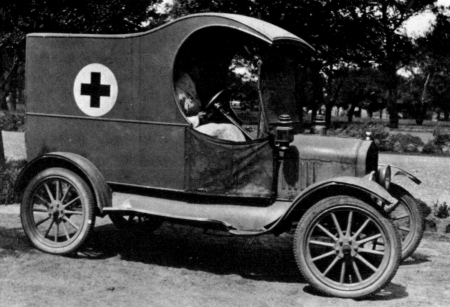

Part of the gathering at the first meeting of lady motorcyclists in Victoria on 27th October 1917. Eventually a run was made to Warrandyte. The tall well-dressed young woman to the left of the picture is none other than the delightful second Switcher at the Empire Theatre.

form, for quite a time but found it a heavy thing to hold up when stationary, leading one of the friendly policemen around to suggest that Miss Nylander might attach a sidecar. This she did, making her life sweeter than ever.

Well, the young woman decided to fill in for Brewster on the film switching business and did it so well that she became the Empire's official Switcher in time, using the Indian for the purpose 'on nights' plus, of all things, driving a little Ford van set out as a Red Cross ambulance during the day. How the shop kept going with Miss Nylander so heavily committed is not known!

Now what attracted Margaret Nylander (Doll, to her friends) to the motorcycle, for she was getting some pretty odd looks from the Brunswick inhabitants who didn't care to see such a nice young woman racing around on a big vee-twin Indian. It was a simple matter, however, and logical enough, for Margaret's parents lived some fifty miles out of Melbourne at a nice little place called Bunyip not served by any means of public transport on a Sunday, when she liked to visit her family. On the round trip of 100 miles, Margaret often had to complete it in the one day, returning to where she boarded in Melbourne on the Sunday evening, ready for business on the Monday. Without the Indian there was just no other way of doing this effectively. However satisfactory this may have been, Margaret's mother was warned that her daughter would become coarse and masculine if she continued to use a motorcycle, but the dear Miss Nylander assured her mother that she would not, and held to it.

Nevertheless, this whole motorcycle business was catching on with the girls, leading to the first meeting of lady motorcyclists in Melbourne on 27th October 1917, with Miss Nylander a leading light in the affair. Mighty interesting women, too, many with academic backgrounds, riding a variety of motorcycles and sidecar outfits. The Melbourne Press revelled in it all and described Margaret as a young old hand who had driven her Indian and sidecar over many miles of Victorian roads, handling her machine with the

Bunyip 1919: Miss Nylander seated on her famous 7hp Powerplus Indian with spring frame. In the sidecar is her niece Edith, then six years old.

technique of an expert. In passing, there's the little story of Mr Harrison, editor of the local sporting paper, who, on one occasion, managed to catch—and catch is the word—Miss Nylander out of motorcycling clothing for a change. Such a unique spectacle caused him to shout across the road to her, 'Why, my dear, I hardly recognized you without your pants.' So be it . . .

Tough and adventurous was our young woman, gamely using her motorcycle and sidecar all the year round, in sad contrast to the men about the place who cared not to use their machines other than in 'comfortable' conditions. Soon the news was around that Miss Nylander, with a lady passenger in her sidecar, planned a genuine 1000-mile trip through the Mallee. Best described as of a forbidding nature, the Mallee was wild territory composed of scrub, with dottings of eucalyptus trees and a total absence of any decent roads but rough dirt tracks that became virtually impassable when the rains came. Covering parts of South Western Australia, New South Wales and Western Australia, the

Mallee occupied an area of some 40,000 square miles, including 17% of the entire State of Victoria.

Undaunted, the young ladies set out from Melbourne via Ballarat, Glenorchy, Lubeck, Rupanyup, Murtoa, Kewell, Dimboola, Jeparit, Rainbow and Yaapeet. While making a tour of the local territory during a stay at Jeparit, another passenger was taken on who decided to remain with the little party to the end of this, the outgoing journey. Now here's something for the record when Miss Nylander, pushing the Indian outfit at quite a lick—three up, remember—completed the 22 miles from Jeparit to Rainbow in 35 minutes on a going of heavy, loose sand.

The idea was to make the return journey to Melbourne via Tarrangyuck to Warracknabeal, Donald, Charlton, Wedderburn, Inglewood, Bendigo and Kyneton, although the locals in those parts said that it would be quite impossible for Miss Nylander to do it because the tracks had broken up following even moderate falls of rain, leaving miles of thick mud, so thick, indeed, that it would constantly jam up between the wheels and mudguards of the outfit. It was usually accepted that for four months of the year the rain made conditions so bad, particularly for motorcyclists, that they just

did not use the tracks here and 'sensibly' stayed away. Not Margaret Nylander, however, who made it back to Melbourne through the shocking conditions then prevailing, although constantly having to stop to clear the mud from the wheels of her machine. Again the Melbourne Press went wild with joy reporting all the details of Miss Nylander's hazardous return journey, and on being interviewed Margaret

During the Melbourne to Sydney Christmas Run, Margaret Nylander pushes the Indian outfit onto Tom Ugly's ferry at Sydney. It was a rule that all vehicles had to be pushed.

The Harley Davidson of 1000cc considered to be both better and stronger than her previous Indian machine; Miss Nylander is seen on the new HD while sister Annie occupies the sidecar originally fitted to the Indian.

The return from Sydney to Melbourne via the South Coast route with the Indian outfit splashing through a semi-submerged bridge constructed of tree trunks.

Another memory of Margaret Nylander's early motorcycling days. Miss Nylander speaking:

'One Saturday night I was going home to my mother's house at Bunyip after I had finished at the Empire Theatre. My brother, who was a returned soldier from the Great War, came with me in the sidecar. After the turn off from the main road, the track that existed was very rough, with potholes everywhere, causing the headlamp to work loose. Being of the acetylene type it naturally just went out, leaving us totally in the dark.

My brother fortunately had a flash-light with him and he held it in a way that would show me the track ahead, although mostly it was shining up in the air or in the bush on the side of the track. The tall trees made everything all the blacker and it was a good thing that I knew the 'road' well. The worst hazard was the kangaroos who crossed in front of us in bunches of twelve to twenty maybe, but they were quite hard to see, particularly if they hopped alongside the outfit and then made a quick dart in front of my wheel. The best thing to do in such circumstances was to stop and let them go. Another worry was the horse drawn vehicles that never had any lights showing and, of course, animals lying in the middle of the road.

The country folk would always stop if I was fixing something, for example, and would want to help me but as they did not know anything about motorcycles I was always afraid that they would touch something that perhaps I might not be able to put right. If I was mending a puncture at the side of the road, near to a house, more than often the owner would bring me some morning or afternoon tea as the case may have been. They were always very kind.'

'Ready to go to Mum's home', 1923. In the sidecar of the Harley Davidson outfit is Margaret's first child Reiwa, born in the wooden house in the background with no doctor in attendance at the time. The location is Tonbinbuck, some seven miles out from Bunyip where large packs of dingos would howl to each other from hill to hill.

stressed in no uncertain way that she considered there was absolutely no reason why a motorcyclist, if he or she fitted a sidecar to a motorcycle, should not use it for 365 days of the year . . . whatever the conditions!

Surprisingly, the Indian that had served Margaret Nylander so well as far as its strictly mechanical reliability was concerned during her more epic rides did, in fact, possess a certain weakness that had caused the owner not a little inconvenience on several occasions. The 'delicate' area of an otherwise very robust machine was the front forks that appeared not to be able to stand the pounding put upon them, particularly on the rougher tracks of Miss Nylander's going. A unique form of front springing the Indian had where a large laminated spring extended forward from an anchorage point about the bottom of the steering head of the main frame to a shackle just above and on a forward part of the mudguard. Plainly that spring was not up to the job required of it and would fracture frequently, no matter how many replacements were fitted over a period. In an attempt to rectify the trouble, the local blacksmith had made up a spring of extra large proportion and although it was as solid as the proverbial rock, it possessed no flexing qualities whatsoever, making a ride on the outfit a very shattering experience.

So, all rather sadly, the famous Indian was detached from its sidecar and sold in 1920 and, taking its place, a more powerful Harley Davidson that had front forks much more to Miss Nylander's liking. Rather ironically, however, the big challenging long distance rides had become a thing strictly of the past. Margaret Nylander was about to be married to an ex-military gentleman, the pair later purchasing a farm only seven miles away from mother's home at Bunyip. The farming venture did not prove to be a success and in the early months of 1924 the couple set up a general store. The Harley Davidson outfit was sold and replaced by a Ford Model T van and all things motorcycle passed out of Margaret Nylander's life.

Cartoonist Roland Davies's view of things. From *The Motor Cycle*, 1928.

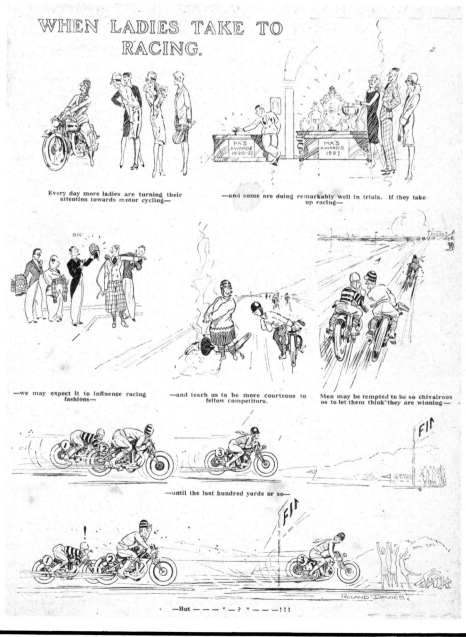

WHEN LADIES TAKE TO RACING.

Every day more ladies are turning their attention towards motor cycling—

—and some are doing remarkably well in trials. If they take up racing—

—we may expect it to influence racing fashions—

—and teach us to be more courteous to fellow competitors.

Men may be tempted to be so chivalrous as to let them think they are winning—

—until the last hundred yards or so—

—But ———"———?———!!!

Moto Vecchia

Lurking in suburban London is an enterprising firm with a passion for Moto Guzzis. DENNIS HOWARD has been to see what they are up to and has delved into the archives to show us some classic shots of old Guzzis in their heyday.

Possessing a near fanatical devotion to Italian motorcycles and engineering, led thirty-four year old Terry Haynes to form a company specializing in the sales and rebuilding of just about any classic machine sired in Italy. His work is thus a labour of love in the truest sense of the word and highly profitable into the bargain.

Called Moto Vecchia, the firm's interests lie in yesterday's motorcycles, and Moto Vecchia when translated

Basically a pre-war design, the Falcone model Moto Guzzi has an interesting history. Although this ex-Police 500cc Falcone of early 1950s vintage appears as anything but a sports machine, Moto-Guzzi works variations gave the once famous Dondolino racing model,

later to be replaced by the Gambalungha (long leg) device, an example of which won the rain-lashed 1948 Ulster Grand Prix at Clady, Enrico Lorenzetti 'up'.

Pictured is an example of Moto Vecchia's restoration of the Falcone in touring trim. Bore and stroke measurements have remained quite constant over many years at 88mm by 82mm respectively. The overhead valves are pushrod operated.

A superb shot of Austrian 250cc Champion 1949–54 Alex Mayer cornering sharply on his quarter litre Moto Guzzi during the progress of a race. Contrary to 500cc Moto Guzzi single cylinder practice during the period of the late 1940s and very early 1950s, the racing 250 machines whether works maintained or privately owned, employed overhead camshaft valve operation. Later to be known as the Gambalunghino (little long leg) as an official production racing 250cc machine, many of the older Albatross 250s (still overhead camshaft) were Gambalunghino'ized and where the Brampton girder front forks were replaced by the very much Guzzi bottom link items, here seen. Carburettor position was also changed. Note the near vertical and indeed large bore Dell'Orto carburettor and the apparent absence of any foot gear change mechanism on Mayer's machine. Although so much of continental origin, the racing Guzzis were fitted with a gear change lever on the English (off-side) side of the machine with the rear brake operating lever on the near side. It would be interesting to learn exactly what gear change system Mayer employed!

into English means Old Bike. It is as simple as that!

Established now for just over three years, Moto Vecchia originally used premises at Thornton Heath, later moving to larger buildings in London's Crystal Palace district and now settled at Colliers Wood, actually just three minutes away from the Underground station on London Transport's Northern Line. Here, in the convivial atmosphere of the Haynes' team thoroughly enjoying their work, motorcycles from such Italian Houses as Parilla, Gilera, CM, Ducati and Aermacchi are either in the process of a super rebuild or may be waiting collection by some enthusiast client. If there exists a slight preference for a particular marque, one gains the impression that Terry Haynes puts the Moto Guzzi in top position, with variations (sporting or touring versions) of the basic 500cc overhead valve Falcone model being a Haynes' speciality. On the other hand, a make never to enjoy the world-wide success story of the Guzzi models, Mr Haynes rates the lesser known MM (Massetti and Morini), a clean-limbed overhead camshaft single cylinder model as an engineer's delight . . . 'so beautifully engineered that the MM literally falls together when a restoration job is required'.

It is certainly strange that in these times of heavy inflation, when classic

Nearside view of the Falcone showing the outside flywheel (a traditional Moto Guzzi feature on most period single cylinder models) which revolved in a clockwise direction. The motor ran backwards to facilitate the geared primary drive.

Note the one-time and indeed typical Guzzi rear suspension system where the chain stays were linked to springs located beneath the gearbox assembly. Damping was supplied by the scissor action units set between the stays and the fixed upper frame member at the rear of the machine.

A Sports version of this Falcone is available from Moto Vecchia which has low racing type handlebars, aluminium wheel rims, plus other niceties in the works department associated with a sporting performance.

A peep inside the Crystal Palace premises workshop with super enthusiasts Stewart Eke and Brett Samson hard at it.

In the middle of the picture a Moto Guzzi Falcone Turismo model is taking shape while nearer the camera a Gilera is in a similar stage of assembly. Every facility exists in the Moto Vecchia works for engine and gearbox overhaul and indeed for frame and fork straightening if necessary. Quality of work and finish is of the very highest standard.

Although aesthetically not so pleasing, the MM machine readily receives full praise by Terry Haynes for the quality of its engineering. This is understandable however for during his club road racing days Mr Haynes owned a superbly made Excelsior Manxman 250 unit (ex Denis Parkinson) neatly fitted into a Doug St John Beasley frame, a top combination if ever there was. To accentuate the point he also raced a Vincent Grey Flash.

Out and about with the Moto Guzzi marque. To the rear is Company founder Terry Haynes seated on a beautifully restored Falcone Turismo model while the writer reflects on the exciting experience that was his, minutes before the picture was taken, riding a very special Guzzi.

The model is a semi-works machine prepared by Moto Guzzi on which Signor Nesono won the Milan to Taranto road race in 1953 covering the 2,800 kilometre course in just twenty hours, at an average speed of approximately 87·5 mph.

The writer described the acceleration of this Guzzi as the most excitingly progressive he had ever encountered on a four stroke single cylinder motorcycle, likening it to a hard thick strand of rubber band untwisting and knowing no end to it all.

A mixture of a road and racing machine fitted with lights, Moto Vecchia intend to produce replicas of the 500cc pushrod operated overhead valve Nesono model which will be called the Sports Special.

The late great Rupert Hollaus pictured at speed on a 250cc Gambalunghino Moto Guzzi at an Austrian race meeting in 1953. This was a very sound and successful design of racing machine, but it had two weaknesses: valve spring breakages and a tendency for the top section of the front fork assembly where it entered the steering head of the frame, to fracture under stress. Later a redesign of the forks cured trouble in that particular department, although Guzzis never quite eliminated the valve spring malady. As a result, a special fitting tool plus a spare valve spring were carried by Moto Guzzi riders in order that an on the spot repair could be effected during a race.

As a works NSU rider in 1954, Hollaus won the 125cc Ultra Lightweight TT and came home in second place in the 250cc Lightweight TT of the year in question.

Italian motorcycles must be accepted as luxury items, the demand on Moto Vecchia is such that the team is sometimes hard-pressed to satisfy all the needs of its enthusiast clients. However the service is second to none with Terry Haynes having to make repeated trips to Italy, often of six weeks' duration, where he must locate further supplies of machines and spares. Fortunately he has built up a large network of contacts in Italy who readily provide him with a suitable location or source of supply of the classic motorcycles. The situation is not easier as time goes by, because negotiating prices become just that little bit higher, though as a sound businessman Mr. Haynes has the sense to realize that one must speculate to accumulate. A comforting thought in this connection is that at the moment Moto Vecchia holds £10,000 worth of spare parts, the supply of which is a very important part of the firm's service to the enthusiast. Generously all part of the Haynes' system . . . 'anything Italian for anybody'.

All smiles as winner of the 1950 Swiss Grand Prix, 250 class, Bruno Ruffo receives his victory laurels. On his works Gambalunghino Moto Guzzi Ruffo had become World Road Racing Champion (250cc) in 1949 and again in 1951. On a 125cc Mondial he also gained the Ultra Lightweight World Championship in 1950. Standing just to Ruffo's left is Umberto Masetti (cooling off with the top half of his racing leathers removed) the famous Gilera works rider who won the 500cc World Road Racing Championship in 1950 and 1952.

By 1952 the 250cc Moto Guzzi had become a very sophisticated device with a more conventional system of rear suspension plus a fuel tank that extended forward of the steering head. On this Gambalunghino model, Fergus Anderson (seated on wall and wearing beret) had won the Lightweight TT at a record speed of 83·82 mph. Ready for a test ride on the Guzzi is former road racer and latterly brilliant technical editor of *The Motor Cycle*, V. H. Willoughby, whose pleasant task it was to write of his impressions of TT winning machines in that particular publication. Alas! Those super days have long since gone.

Former editor of *The Motor Cycle*, Harry Louis (extreme left), appears totally seduced by the Guzzi . . . a quite understandable situation!

Social Workshop

In those glorious days of long ago, when the town and country were decently separated and when the sun shone when it should, GUY ASHENDEN had a small problem, a sprained knee and an unserviceable motorcycle. This was his amusing solution . . .

Browned off, that's what I was, sitting up in bed alone in the house on a fine Saturday afternoon about a fortnight before Easter 1930. My left knee was swollen up like a prize vegetable marrow at a garden fête following a severe sprain when playing rugger a week before. My parents had gone to play bridge some miles away and were not likely to return to the Ashenden homestead before supper—or so I thought. I had a big stack of Blue'uns

and Green'uns (affectionate reference to the publications *The Motor Cycle* and *Motor Cycling*) to read, plus several records of what I recall might be referred to as of a cheerful nature, spinning their way in turn on my portable gramophone.

For all this, however, I was still browned off, not just on account of being shut up indoors in good weather, or indeed the sprained knee, for it seemed more than likely that I should

not be fit in time to take part in my little gang's usual Easter run to North Devon. Furthermore, my 350 Zenith/JAP badly needed a top end

A recent photograph of the author seated on his 1924/26, 348cc Henley Blackburne.

Purchased by Guy Ashenden in 1937 for £3, the Henley is now used mainly for personal transport although it has a racing history of not a little interest.

29

overhaul including new valve guides, and even if my knee had recovered in time I just could not see how I could get the engine done as well.

A somewhat unorthodox solution to the problem began to form in my mind when I heard the burbling, purring exhaust note of Jack Stannard's Scott Squirrel two-speeder pulling up by our front gate. My mother had left the front door on the latch in case of probable visitors and now here was Jack running up the stairs.

'How's the leg you poor old ruin?'— a typical Stannard greeting.

'Ruddy painful,' said I and then proceeded to pour out all my troubles.

'H'um, not much you can do about it is there?' said J.S.

'Well I don't know,' I said slowly, 'my people won't be back until about 7.30 and there's a big stack of old newspapers in the kitchen cupboard and it wouldn't take you more than fifteen minutes to go down to my shed and whip the Zenith's cylinder head off . . . would it?'

Stannard stared at me as though I might be mad. 'You don't mean that you are thinking of decoking the thing IN BED, do you?'

'I don't see why not, and with newspapers it wouldn't make any mess . . . you can bring me a bowl of hot water and the "Gresolvent" to have a wash afterwards. Why! The job shouldn't take more than an hour at the most.'

'Ye gods,' replied Jack, 'I have always thought you were scatty—now I know you most certainly are! What on earth would your people say?'

'There's absolutely no reason at all why they should ever know anything about it . . . I can get it done and you can get it screwed back together well before they get home. Go on,' I said, 'be a pal. The valve spring compressor is in the bench drawer, also the valve grinding sucker thing, and all the spanners you will need are hanging on the wall.'

In somewhat of a daze Jack Stannard descended the stairs while I selected a suitable record 'of a cheery nature' and felt all rather good about things at last. About half an hour later Jack returned with the JAP's cylinder head, all necessary tools for the operation plus a vast heap of newspapers under his arm.

I had just removed the valves when we heard the deep thumping note of Dick Cumming's Anzani-engined Aero Morgan pulling up outside, followed by a snuffling, gasping noise as Dick's nearly spherical 12-stone Golden Labrador accelerated up the stairs.

'That's the lowest geared dog I've ever known,' said Jack. 'About time they gave the poor old beast a spot of exercise.'

The spherical Bruce pushed the bedroom door open with his nose and

Jack Stannard
on Scott Squirrel.

followed his usual practice when entering any bedroom of climbing directly onto the bed all in one style of very smooth movement. Fortunately, my bed was a fairly large double one and I was able to hoist my damaged leg out of the dog's way just in the nick of time. Following Bruce came Dick's sister. Now I suppose in these days of hackneyed phrases and stereotyped descriptions Sylvia Cummings would be catalogued as 'Blonde, smashing, 34–23–33 and so on'. Tony Wilson-Brown, Secretary of the West Kent MCC perhaps offered the best description of Sylvia from a motorcyclist's point of view by suggesting that she possessed smoother lines than a cammy Chater-Lea. However, if you

have not seen one, you probably cannot appreciate fully the aptness of the simile. As girls go, Sylvia Cummings was certainly a 'one-off' job.

The lovely creature stood transfixed, gazing at my filthy hands and the JAP cylinder head, while Dick looking over her shoulder said, 'Well, you ticked me off last week for re-enamelling my wheels in the kitchen, Sis. What do you think of this for enthusiasm then?'

'Enthusiasm!!! I have never seen anything so horrible in my life, Guy. How can you, and what on earth would your mother say?'

'Look old thing,' I said, 'I've been through all of this with Jack before you and Dick turned up. Everything is under control and the job will certainly

a home,' before settling herself down to read.

'Look Jack,' I've just realized that I am out of valve grinding paste. Would you care to jump on the old model and nip down the road to Dalton-Stephens and get a tin? There's some small change in that old timing case cover on the mantelpiece.'

'Fair enough,' said Jack, 'I'll be back in a few minutes.'

We listened entranced as that Scott's glorious 'yowl' rose to a musical crescendo before fading into the distance. However, no sooner had Jack gone than we heard the rorty arrival of Bunny Lynn's Model 18 Norton outfit complete with Ted Evans, Bunny's regular sidecar passenger.

'Ye gods, what a crush ... Sylvia you look like a box of Turkish Delight! Very edible indeed! As for that dog of yours, Dick, it must be running at about eighty pounds per square inch. You really should put a tyre gauge on him for if he gets any fatter he'll blow you all to pieces before long.' Bunny always spoke his mind thus.

Meanwhile, Ted was surveying the scene of activity. 'I've always wanted to do a top end overhaul in bed,' he said enviously ... 'as it is, my old bag of a landlady won't even let me do it in the yard.... Oh! By the way, you really should have seen that lunatic Stannard screaming down Bromley Common on that Scott of his just now ... He must have been doing a good sixty when he passed us. Butch and Fungus-mug will have him in their lousy trap sure as fate being a Saturday afternoon!'

These events taking place before the days of mobile police, it should be explained that Butch and Fungus-mug were the sergeant and constable who worked the almost regular weekend speed trap on that particular road.

'He'll be OK,' said Dick. 'My fiancée works in the Police HQ, as you know. She told me at lunch-time that Butch is off duty—got a ruddy great boil on his backside; can't ride his bike. They're too short-handed to replace him, so the trap won't be in action.'

''bout time. The miserable old devil nicked me for thirty bob last week! Said I was doing 80! That old Ajay of mine wouldn't do more than 65, even if you were to chuck it over Beachy Head. Hope his boil blows him out of bed!'

Sylvia put the Blue'un down. 'You really are a disgusting beast, Ted! The poor man must be in agony! Pity you don't get a boil or two yourself; you'd be a bit more sympathetic.'

'I shouldn't! Serves him damn-well right! The ignorant old toad can't even read a stop-watch properly. Hope he gets one on his nose as well!'

'I think motorcyclists are the most callous lot of brutes I've ever met,' said Sylvia.

The Scott spluttered to a halt outside. Jack came in and threw me the tin of Carborundum paste. 'Here,' he said, 'you'll have to fit the new guides before you grind in the valves. Where are they?'

'Oh, on the shelf above the bench. You'll have to put 'em in for me, and you can't do it out there, because of the place next door. Bring 'em up, and the old orange box that's full of rag on the hut floor; you can stand it here in the hearth and use it as a bench to knock 'em in.'

'What,' asked Bunny, 'is the place next door?'

'A maternity home. They've about 50 newborn brats in there. I don't dare make the slightest sound in the hut in the afternoon; it brings that frightful old dragon of a matron round banging on the front door. The little perishers all wake up together. It's like a massed start for blown two-strokes at Brooklands—ghastly row!'

Sylvia slammed the Blue'un down on the bed. 'Little perishers indeed! Don't be so perfectly foul! Newborn babies are adorable ... !'

'Well,' I said, eyeing her appreciatively, 'I dare say a few of 'em in about seventeen years' time. ...'

'You looked like they do once, and what's more, you've not changed a lot—not mentally at least, otherwise you wouldn't be overhauling your bike in bed!'

Jack came in with orange box, valve guides and a brass drift. I gave him the head. 'You brought the carb' up, didn't you?'

'Yes. Here it is.'

'Sling it over to Ted. Ted, give it a look over will you? Just see if the jets are clear.'

'OK. Let's have it.'

The room became quite thick with smoke from Bunny's foul pipe.

'You know,' he said, puffing thoughtfully, 'one reads of the tuning wizards down at Brooklands with their little huts, all with notices on the door saying: KEEP OUT—THIS MEANS YOU etc, and there they are alleged to perform miracles of speed in their miserable solitude. Personally I think it's the wrong attitude altogether. Give me a social workshop every time, like this! Beautiful feminine scenery, the chief tuner doing his stuff in bed in perfect comfort, all his pals around him giving a hand—and so on.'

The catchy rhythm of a spot of ukelele playing from the gramophone had Ted snapping his fingers and dancing away over by the window, while Jack handed me the cylinder head, where I smeared paste on the exhaust valve, and began to twiddle it on its seating with the sucker.

And so dear reader of the nineteen-eighties, you who probably earn a big enough screw to have your large capacity multi-cylinder job with its totally enclosed valve gear and care-

be finished before my parents get home. Now there are several Roddy and Lavinda stories in these Blue'uns that you may not have read, so shove that elephantine hound of yours a bit further over. Take a pew on the end of the bed and get stuck in—I know Lavinda is one of your current heroines.'

The stories about Lavinda, her 350 Dot-Bradshaw and boyfriend Roddy were written by E. Carey-Riggall and appeared regularly in *The Motor Cycle*. In those days such stories were our favourite fiction.

Sylvia required no further encouragement and picked up a handful of copies, took one more look at my hands and said, 'You should be put in fully designed inaccessibility, overhauled by your local agent if you are laid up in bed, I ask you just to try to visualize the scene that met my parents' gaze when the door of my bedroom slowly—and so VERY unexpectedly—opened on that sunny Saturday afternoon so many years ago.

The room was thick with smoke, the colossal dog had turned on his back with all four legs pointing to the ceiling, and the decorative Sylvia absentmindedly scratched his stomach while she read. I was sitting up in bed, a smear of graphite grease on my face, coal black hands grinding in my valves, the gramophone blaring out at maximum revs. Bunny stood by the fireplace puffing his filthy pipe, Jack sat on the floor reading the Green'un, Ted was fiddling with the Amac carburettor on the orange box, Dick sat on my only bedroom chair reading: 'Speed—and How to Obtain It'—and in my parents came! Bless 'em, they seized up solid, both physically and verbally, in their best go-to-party togs; there they stood—rooted to the spot!

Bunny saw 'em first; he moved over and took the needle off the record. The silence was ghastly!

'W-what,' asked my mother, in a very small voice, 'is going on?'

'B-but,' I answered, 'why are you back so soon? I thought you'd gone over to Sidcup. Didn't expect you for another three hours at least!'

'Evidently! Well, Mrs Claughton has influenza, and as neither of us is on the 'phone, she couldn't let us know. We had to wait ages for a bus to get back. But what on earth's that filthy great thing on your lap? And look at your hands, and the bed! It's broken through the paper and is all over the sheet—and on the pillow behind your head! **Really!** I've never in all my life . . .'

Sylvia looked at her with deep compassion, 'I know Mrs A., I've tried to stop them. He wants to get his bike ready for Easter. Dick's nearly as bad; he was painting his wheels in the kitchen last week. Mother nearly went mad! By the time we got here it had gone too far. They said they'd get it done well before you got back, or I'd never have let them start it!'

'I'd like to have seen you stop us!'

My father broke in. 'But this is the bitter end! These beastly motor-bikes are an absolute obsession! Upon my living soul I've never seen such a disgusting scene in all my life—you really have gone too far this time!'

'Look, Dad. If you'd had a motor-cycle when you were my age . . .'

'The foul death-engines hadn't been invented, thank God! Even if they had, I would not have owned one even as a gift! Always going wrong. They make a frightful row, and a worse mess, and as for overhauling it IN BED!'

'Well, what about that first pony you had then? What was the story Uncle

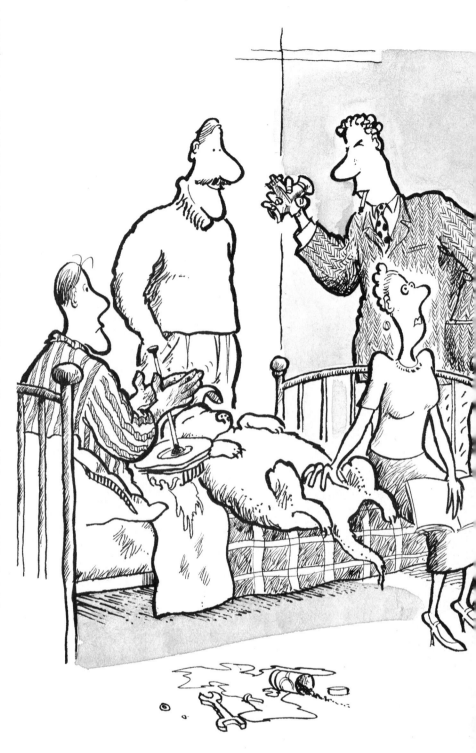

Fred used to tell about the time you wanted to clip it, and they wouldn't let you go out in the stable because you had a cold, so you sneaked out and brought it into the drawing-room through the french windows. You were clipping it in there when a violent thunderstorm sent the poor little beast berserk; it kicked half the Chippendale into matchwood and turned the new Axminster into a fair replica of a stable yard . . .'

'Well, I was only twelve! You're twenty-two, and overhauling the blasted thing IN BED . . .'

There arose a peculiar gurgling noise

rather like bathwater running out, which changed to a maniacal cackle. I've known Ted Evans' laugh set a whole cinema audience going, and they'd no idea what had amused him. Sylvia had a handkerchief stuffed in her mouth. My mother saw it, and sat down weakly on the filthy orange box that Ted had been using as a bench.

All eight of us succumbed, completely and utterly. Bruce sat up on the bed and barked his head off. Dick wound a towel round his head and calmed him down.

'M-Mrs A.,' sobbed Sylvia. 'You must be t-tired after g-going all the w-

way to S-Sidcup and b-back by b-bus, and y-you've had no t-tea. S-shall I go and make some?'

'P-please, dear. Oh! my dreadful, dreadful son! What'll you get up to next?'

It was quite a party. Well, after all, one could hardly call it a social workshop without the odd 'cuppa' now could you? That vast dog devoured a complete fruit cake without anyone noticing him, and I got the head finished, and Jack screwed it all back together.

So I went on the run to Devon. It rained like hell all the way there and

most of the way home. Jack had two punctures and the Moggie threw a pushrod into a thick hedge at about 1 a.m., somewhere near Frome on the return journey. We pushed the Morgan half a mile and left it in a barn leaving a note on the driving seat. 'Will fetch next weekend,' and we did.

Sylvia had returned home in Bunny's sidecar with Ted on the Norton's pillion. I had no pillion seat so Dick sat on my saddle and I sat on the Zenith's tank, the former operating the long gear change lever on the Sturmey gearbox, while I worked the clutch as and when n´cessary. This

system worked perfectly until about 3 a.m. Dick failed to concentrate on what he was obliged to do and shoved the machine into bottom instead of top at about 40 m.p.h.

Now one may talk about the merits of disc brakes in a modern setting, yet here was I immediately hanging over the handlebars looking directly into the gas headlamp, while Dick slid up onto my back before we both rolled slowly over into a muddy ditch . . . ! But all that is another story . . . HAPPY DAYS!

PRE-WAR CLUBMAN

His Life and Times

Norman Sanderson was born in Finchley, North London, in 1915 and subsequently became a pupil of the now defunct Finchley High School. After taking a business training course when his schooling was completed, he joined the staff of the London office of W. M. Christy and Sons, the Lancashire towel manufacturers, in 1933.

During the war years the writer served with the 1st London Divisional Provost Company Corps of Military Police under the command of the late Sir Malcolm Campbell, later transferring to the King's Royal Rifle Corps.

Norman Sanderson rejoined his old firm after the war, where he became heavily involved on the sales side of the business. It was at this period that he married and also found time to write his 1930s motorcycling memoirs that are now made available to readers after more than three decades of comparative hibernation.

On completion of forty-two years service with Christy and Sons, Norman Sanderson recently retired and now he and his wife plus the newly-acquired and already much loved Yorkshire Terrier, Teddy, live in the peaceful little Suffolk village of Cavendish. In the writer's words 'A place where people still find time to actually speak to each other'.

My introduction to the motorcycling scene came in 1930 when I was fifteen years of age. A friend asked me to go with him to London's Olympia Motorcycle Show, particularly as he was contemplating buying a 150cc Coventry-Eagle two-stroke and wished to examine in detail the model on the Coventry-Eagle stand. I must confess that at the time I had no interest whatsoever in motorcycles and consequently knew nothing about them, but I agreed to go along just to keep the peace as it were.

However I had not been at Olympia very long before I realized that motorcycling was going to be my way of life to a great degree and I returned home with that conclusion firmly set in my mind. Reason prevailed however, presenting the not insignificant consideration that motorcycles cost money and they certainly did, even in the 1930s. Be that as it may, my big chance came in 1931 when casually peeping through the window of a neighbour's garage I spied an old motorcycle standing against the wall. I asked the owner if he would be prepared to sell it, upon which he asked me how much I would pay for it. Without blushing I offered ten shillings, being my total funds, and like a sportsman he accepted, remarking that the machine was thoroughly sound but had no clutch. Having no mechanical knowledge I asked him if the absence of a clutch really mattered much, to which he replied that the fitment was certainly an asset to the greater enjoyment of motorcycling although he had managed very well without it.

I did not appreciate the value of a clutch until I took my first ride, when after getting away by running the machine, leaping into the saddle and engaging gear with an almighty clunk, I found myself confronted by a policeman who made gestures indicating that I should immediately stop. After a moment's reflection I realized that this would be quite impossible and I shouted to him to get out of the way. That policeman must be given full marks for he stood his ground until the last possible moment and then leapt for it in no uncertain manner. I can only assume that this hurried exit saved me from a summons as he obviously had no time to read my rather indistinct number plates as he went.

If a mystery so far as to the actual machine I now owned—it was in fact a 1921 Coulson-Blackburne with a leaf spring frame, 2 speeds, belt drive, while the powerhouse was a 350cc side valve unit with a large outside flywheel. As I have already mentioned I did not have the mechanical knowledge at this time to understand fully the ways of a motorcycle as far as its working systems were concerned, but

I intended to learn as much as I could by stripping the Blackburne engine down before using the machine regularly on the road. I can honestly say that I learnt much more in the time taken on the overhaul than I had previously done from my various books on the subject. True to the previous owner's sales advice, the engine was in very good condition and I used the Coulson for quite a time before selling it to my brother for one pound. Reflecting on my Coulson days I am somewhat amazed that the insur-

ance company ever took on my business particularly as I told the truth on the proposal form about how much the machine cost me, being considerably less than the premium rate.

My next possession was a 350cc side valve BSA of 1924 vintage and all the luxury with chain drive, three speed gearbox and 'Thank Heavens', a clutch. Quite a neat package for £4 10s.

Although still at school, I was now rapidly learning all about motorcycle lore and in fact I thought so much about motorcycles that one day during a Maths lesson my mind wandered to such a degree that my obvious far away look attracted the master to call: 'Sanderson, what would you do . . .', to which I replied 'I would decarbonize it Sir'. If this remark caused howls of mirth from my classmates, it very nearly brought about howls of a very different nature from me when I received six of the best for my very 'brilliant' reply.

Following the BSA I became the proud owner of a 1928 350cc overhead

My first competitive motorcycling event, the London-Land's End Trial 1935. Alas! failure on the 'Beggar's Roost' section while riding the little 250cc overhead valve BSA.

valve New Imperial. Proud is the operative word with now an ohv job (progress indeed) that had a proper saddle tank, internal expanding brakes AND twist grip throttle control instead of the old lever business. The New Imp was a very sporting mount purchased for £9 and with it I saw quite a lot of England. About this time I became interested in watching trials

The very special excitement of owning one's first brand new motorcycle. The writer is shown seated on his 1936 Model 36/16 AJS 350 fitted with coil ignition.

and speed events of one kind or another although not yet belonging to a Club.

Permit me here to digress for a moment. My brother, who remains to this day a great car enthusiast, owned in 1933 a model J2 MG Midget which he entered for sporting club events. He once took my father to see some relatives in this car. Father had no knowledge of cars and never drove one throughout his life and on arriving at the destination was asked how he enjoyed the trip. He said that it had been quite pleasant although my brother drove far too fast and every

time he had looked up he observed that they had been doing '80'. It turned out that the old chap had been looking at the oil pressure gauge!

Incidentally my brother had the name 'OTAZADES' painted on each side of his MG's bonnet and Father who was a churchwarden showed more than a little concern about the choice of name for the car. However it all ended well when the lady next door told my mother that she thought 'OTAZADES' was such a pretty gipsy name chosen for the vehicle in question. She could have been kidding!

My next motorcycle was a 1932 250cc BSA with overhead valves and it was in very nice condition. On this mount I commenced my competitive motorcycling by entering for the London–Land's End Trial of 1935, an

event organized by the Motor Cycling Club. I sent in my entry form quite early but was surprised to find later that my starting number was '2'. How pleased I felt that I had not been number 1 in my very first trial. On arriving at the start at Virginia Water in Surrey I was awed by the large crowd that had assembled to see us start off on our long ride. I kept looking round anxiously waiting for number 1 to arrive but as the minutes ticked by he failed to materialize and then to my horror I heard it announced that he was a non-starter and I should be first away.

Perhaps you can imagine how I felt as some important personage shook my hand and wished me good luck while photographs were taken of me simply because I was first man off.

Never, but never, have I felt more pleased to get moving than I did on that night forty-six years ago. I need not dwell on the trial itself except to say that I failed every section except one which I managed to foot my way up after a struggle. However I did finish, so at least I felt I had achieved something. I shall never forget a nightingale singing in some woods and my first sight of dawn over Exmoor after tackling Doverhay being the first observed section of the trial, in the dark. These things alone made me want to have another shot at the next Land's End Trial.

One rather amusing incident occurred at the finish when a reporter asked me to give him my story of the run. I explained that he should ask one of the experienced competitors who no doubt would have done well, but apparently as I finished first he thought that I had 'won the race' and insisted on me giving him as much information as possible. This was a bright spot in the proceedings, however, for my brother had entered the trial in his MG but retired with a burnt-out clutch on one of the Somerset sections. I say bright spot, for otherwise I should have been severely ragged for my poor performance. As it was my magneto failed in the middle of Exeter on the homeward journey but fortunately I was able to find a garage with the necessary parts to get the item operating again. I must say that in those days a truly wonderful spirit of comradeship existed among the competitors and many were the friendly smiles I received as I was passed by other riders on more powerful machines on their own particular way back from Land's End.

Shortly after this trial I was temporarily *hors de combat* following the removal of my appendix and during this time of enforced non-motorcycling activity I saved as hard as my wages permitted in those days and eventually purchased my first new machine a model 36/16 350cc ohv AJS. When this plot was properly run in I joined a club which proved to be a turning-point in my motorcycling life. Here I met good friends all sharing a common interest and learned a lot from the more experienced members. During the summer months I tuned the AJS to the best of my ability and entered it for the Club's Speed Hill Climb which was run twice a year over private ground, the course being about a quarter of a mile in length.

I thoroughly enjoyed this event although I am afraid that my machine was not quite a match for the camshaft Velocettes in the 350cc class. My AJS also transported me to the Isle of Man to view the 1936 TT races. I went over for Race Week (not the practice period) and can honestly assure any enthusiast who has yet to see his first TT that it is a spectacle he will never forget. I stood near the foot of Bray Hill, which as some of you may know is a short way down from the start/finish area. When the first machine appeared over the brow of the hill and hurtled down towards me, I realized at once that compared to this, my own riding ability was absolutely nil and I left after the race feeling completely awed. Quite apart from the races, the scenery is magnificent and the island takes a lot of beating in my opinion, as a holiday resort.

In the Autumn of 1936 I entered the AJS for a sporting trial our Club was organizing. I was not using competition tyres and in all truth I must have departed from the model at least fifteen times before the finish although, thank goodness, not always in an observed section. When the results were announced I found that I had won a bronze medal, the lowest award in the trial which anybody could win. To this day I prize this medal more than any other I possess.

In 1937 I bought myself a new 350cc Tiger 80 Triumph. I cannot speak too highly of this particular machine. It was entered in trials, speed hill climbs, scrambles, sprint events and even raced at Brooklands before I sold it, with a heavy heart at the end of 1938 during which time it had shared many adventures with me, some of which I would wish to tell you about.

Easter 1937 and once again I faced the starter of the London–Land's End Trial. This time I did not feel so nervous as I had done in 1935, knowing more or less the form and what to expect. There is a definite something about these long-distance trials which is certainly not to be found in other events. For one thing they test the man as well as the machine for in the case of the Land's End event, by starting on the evening of Good Friday, one has to ride all night without sleep before tackling Doverhay, previously mentioned, the first observed hill ascent near Porlock in Somerset.

Thus it will be realized that the competitor is tired even before the serious part of the trial begins. To provide an example, on this occasion I was riding in close company with two very good friends of mine mounted on Velocettes. I brought up the rear of the trio and suddenly somewhere in Cornwall the leader went round a sharp left-hand bend all rather too quickly. The second man just got round it almost on that proverbial ear, but by the time I arrived there was no time to do anything but just go straight on across the road, slap into the grass bank and not really helping the Tiger at all. I mention this episode for while in no way excusing myself for this lapse of fine concentration, such a thing would have been most unlikely to happen had the rider felt fresh and consequently more alert. Anyhow I finished the trial once again and this time managed to get a bronze medal because I made some clean ascents of several hills, under observation.

Ah well! this to me was a step in the right direction. Perhaps next year . . . who knows. Later in the year I entered the Tiger in our own Speed Hill Climb, an event to which I briefly referred a little earlier in my story. A slight description of the hill might assist one to understand what the riders were called upon to face. The event worked on an electrically timed basis and from the starting line the hill went straight up between overhanging trees for 180 yards or so before competitors came upon a left-hand hairpin bend which called for skill in negotiating. Once round this bend the hill increased in steepness with a fast right-hand curve up to the finish line.

This year the surface was loose and therefore the start was tricky and if the rider gave his machine too much throttle, combined with bad clutch work, he found himself in difficulties right away losing precious time in consequence. Never did I realize until then how much just one second meant in an event of this nature. Awards were sometimes won by fractions of a second from other riders, so a good start was essential for success. Now come up the hill with me in your imagination. You are waiting on the line, the green light shows up and you are off. Careful, not too much throttle, keep well back on the rear pad, mind that clutch operation or it will set you back timewise. Right, now give her all she has got, change into second gear and flatten yourself down on the bike's fuel tank in order to reduce wind resistance. A racing gear change into third and get ready to brake for the hairpin bend; on with the brakes and down into second, down into first, round the hairpin, change up again into second and flat out with it before going into third gear with the machine heeled well over to the right while you make this change. Again, press yourself well down on the tank top until you cross the finishing line. It seems ages since you were at the start but when the announcer gives your time 'over the air' for the climb as 27·5 seconds, this brings you back to reality. At this meeting I was fortunate enough to get a 'second fastest time' in the 350cc class, thus entitling me to an award.

In September 1937 I entered my 350cc Triumph for the Motor Cycling Club's High Speed Trials at Brooklands. This was to be my first experience of the famous Track and I spent a long time getting the engine in as near perfect mechanical condition as possible. I polished the cylinder head and ports by hand for hours until they were really smooth. I also managed to secure a secondhand Brooklands' silencer which had sat on the tail end of some other Brooklands' bike at one time or another. The carburation received much attention and the whole motorcycle was fussed over to the very best of my ability. The   a funny story surroun   -
lands pr   s
worth   e
Tr
s
there
down a local by-
when it was reasona   believe me, I hate motes'   ng
undue noise on the roa
bad for the motorcycling
did feel justified on th   n
trying out the bike. I w   -
ing a roundabout at the s
when a policeman suddenly   out from behind some bushes and promptly signalled me to stop (shades

of my Coulson-Blackburne days). I did so this time, however, feeling pretty bad inside although outwardly keeping very calm. He said he thought that my machine was not equipped with a standard silencer with suitable baffle plates etc, and I, putting on an expression as a hurt saint said I was sure it must be legal as I had never received a complaint before. The constable then produced a length of steel which he worked through the fish-tail of my Brooklands Can, eventually looking up with a puff of triumph on his face. At this point I just could not continue my pretence any longer so I told him the truth and explained that the machine was being raced at Brooklands in a few days' time and I was testing it out. To my utter amazement his reply went something like this . . . 'Why the devil didn't you tell me this before because I don't mind you genuine enthusiasts; its them Promenade Percies I hate! The policeman then shook my hand and wished me luck and I saw quite a lot of him after that always in a very friendly capacity. Boy! Was that a relief, and thinking about it I suppose I just happened to be an enthusiast not known on his patch.

The day of the Brooklands meeting duly arrived and I had fitted an engine sprocket to the Triumph with one tooth more than standard as I could not bring myself to attempt to hold the Tiger flat out for an hour with standard gearing. The machines in this High Speed Trial had to be fully equipped with lighting sets that worked; in other words they were in standard trim with the exception of the Brooklands Can.

I had entered as a member of a team with the two lads I mentioned who rode Velocettes in the Land's End Trial. We were allowed to practise in the morning for a short period and during this time my silencer split, owing to vibration. Naturally this was rather a blow and as I could not get hold of another one in sufficient time, it meant that I should have to use a standard silencer with due alterations to suit the carburettor's jet size, etc. However, the job was eventually done and as starting-time approached it began to rain, nasty fine stuff which made things rather unpleasant. Anyhow, at length we were away and I began to realize soon enough how terribly bumpy the track was particularly when one was riding a machine with a rigid frame. Sometimes I was shot off the rear pad and when just about to resume my normal position, the bike would hit another bump and clout me once more. After about ten laps of this going I was horrified to find that my oil pressure-gauge showed no pressure at all. At this, all kinds of unpleasant thoughts ran through my mind with my wondering if the oil pump had failed and the consequent seizure of my engine. I kept my left hand at the ready to whip out the

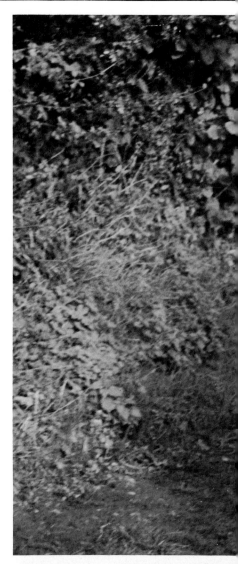

The much loved Triumph Tiger 80 model doing well in the hands of its owner on 'Jacob's Ladder' in the Lockhart-Bossingham Trial, 1937. This event was organised by the very active Berkhamsted Motorcycle and Car Club.

The author indulging in one of his favourite speed events, being the Hill Climb at Dancer's End, Tring, Herts. Still with the Triumph 350 for the 1938 season.

clutch at the slightest signs of protest from the engine. If I had not been a member of a team I should certainly have slowed down, but I felt that I must not let the others down if I could possibly keep going. In spite of the apparent lack of oil pressure the Triumph's engine seemed as sweet as ever and after a while I realized that whatever was wrong, the oil supply was reaching all parts of the engine requiring vital lubrication.

Soon after this, every time I banked the machine onto the Home Banking the engine would cut out for a short distance and then resume its healthy roar once again. No doubt this was caused by water getting on the sparking plug when the machine was heeled over, near to the wet track, for it happened regularly on every lap until the finish. I had no idea of my speed as I had long since lost count of just how many laps I had covered. When eventually the results were given however I was very pleased to learn that I had obtained a Premier Award and that we had won one of the Team prizes. I think this speaks volumes for the Triumph Tiger battling on in standard trim under such conditions to average 65·44mph. At a later date when I stripped the bike's engine down I found that the pipe to the oil pressure gauge had fractured thereby causing the 'no pressure indicated' business on the gauge itself.

I entered the Triumph for a trial, run by a neighbouring club at Christmas 1937 and after a really enjoyable day out found that I had made best motorcycle performance. Oh! How I came to love that bike as time went by and nothing but nothing would have induced me to part with it for the 1938 season of events shortly to come!

When writing of 1938 events, I think it ____ confusing if I describe b____ Hill Climbs together. T____ in May and September ____ and by this time I was ____ how the best way of ____ ill. The star riders always ____ the inside of the hairpin ____ never took it wide on the out____ Time was saved by going more sl____ the inside of the bend ____elling faster and taking ____ I adopted this tactic and ____ engine sprocket with one ____ standard and of course ____ lowering the respective ge____ios for this climb. I entered two classes at the May meeting for 350cc and 500cc Sports machines and won

them both. The Tiger 80 was motoring beautifully that day and everything seemed just right with the bike. The times for the classes respectively were 26·2 seconds, and 26·9 seconds over the quarter-mile hill from a standing start. The Tiger had every reason to feel pleased with its performance that day for the climb in 26·2 seconds was a record for the 350cc Sports Class.

In the September meeting I entered both the 350cc Sports and Racing classes plus the 500cc Sports Class. Whatever, the machine still appeared to be tuned correctly for this event as it won the 350cc Sports Class with a run in 26·9 seconds while getting a second place in both the other classes so entered. Entered in my 'log' went the comment 'quite a creditable day for the old bus once again'.

During the year a run to the Vincent HRD works at Stevenage in Hertfordshire was arranged by our Club and most of the motorcycle members turned up for this, particularly as we had been promised a ride on the 998cc twin cylinder Rapide model. What a day as we impatiently waited our turn to sample this real road 'gobbler'. When it came to my time to ride the Rapide, I set out along the Great North Road and was amazed at the effortless way in which the machine just ate up the miles. During my return run to the factory I really got down to it and was able to achieve my ambition of doing the magic 100 miles per hour on a motorcycle.

An interesting fact resulting from this grand afternoon's enjoyment was that in the four hours during which we had used this Rapide it covered 240 miles, including the changing over of riders and short chats with each man about its performance. This speaks for itself without any elaboration from me. May I say 'thank you very much Mr Vincent for helping me to achieve my ambition in more ways than one'.

Easter 1938 and another crack at the London–Land's End Trial. If you recall, this event had been my first attempt at any form of competitive motorcycling and I so wished to conquer the not informidable hills set out in this Trial, and so to obtain a Premier Award. Well this time I did it and got my 'Premier'. Perhaps you will understand the satisfaction this gave me when I looked back to my first attempt and compared my performances on the then and now basis. Experience had taught me in the interval quite a few things, one being that it was easier to control the machine on a section while standing on the footrests than just sitting iin the saddle.

The Motorcycling Club (MCC) holds three really classic events every year being in order the Land's End

Trial (Easter), the Edinburgh Trial at Whitsuntide and finally the Exeter Trial, run about the Christmas period. Back in 'my' pre-war motorcycling days should a competitor so wish, he could hold back on his Premier Award in the Land's End Trial and try for the Club's Triple Award which was given to those who obtained a Premier Award in all three trials of the same year. As I had been lucky enough to get my Premier Award in the Land's End Trial, I decided to try this year for the Triple Award and at Whitsuntide found myself facing the starter in my first Edinburgh Trial on a section of the Great North Road just a little way up from Barnet. About five minutes after starting off on the long run to Scotland it began to rain and continued to do so throughout the night ride part of the event, all the way North. I believe this must have been one of the most severe Edinburgh Trials ever held for on one or two hills the delays were considerable. As you may know, these trials are run to a time schedule and any competitor arriving late at a check point loses any chance of winning an award. To make matters worse there were secret checks so that no rider knew of his exact situation. I had just climbed the first observed section of this trial 'clean', but on descending the hill after it I skidded and hit a gate. As a result of this encounter with quite a substantial piece of wood, I bent the bike's headlamp and broke the glass; and as I was not early even then, I worked feverishly to tidy things up a bit before proceeding. If my memory serves me correctly the trial was run at an average speed of 27mph and any delay meant that a competitor would have to go all out to maintain a chance of gaining an award.

I shall not easily forget that ride through winding Yorkshire lanes and up the Pennine passes, but I did reclaim my time deficit and that was all that really mattered. One of the last sections in Scotland was really tricky where competitors had to cross a stream which in normal times would not have presented any problem but the rain had turned this into a raging torrent. As the entrant just in front of me attempted the crossing he fell off his machine which promptly disappeared under the water. How my heart went out to him and indeed how also it beat faster when I thought of what might happen to me at any moment. Anyhow, by keeping the motor revving hard which I did by slipping the clutch, I managed to get through without trouble. There was a muddy bank on the other side of this 'stream' where the rider had to stop his machine as the observed section started there. It really was nasty and how I ever managed to climb this section cleanly still remains something of a mystery to me. A close friend told me later that after this section he was cracking along

A twenty-three year old Norman Sanderson, happy as a box of birds, takes his Tiger 80 through an uphill section in the '38 London-Land's End Trial. In this event he gained a Premier Award.

at a fairly rapid rate and, when approaching a sharp bend in the road, found to his dismay that his brakes were not functioning properly, probably due to water in the drums. He just got round but scraped the bank on the wrong side of the road in so doing. I learnt a lesson through this incident which is well worth remembering and that is to always test one's brakes immediately after riding through deep water.

I eventually reached the finish in Edinburgh, wet through after a tiring but very enjoyable trial. Later when the results were given, the official ones, I found that I had got my Premier Award. As only one other solo machine

in the entry of nearly 200 managed to do this, I felt very pleased indeed and I was still in a position to try for my Triple Award.

And so on to the Exeter Trial. It was the first of these classic Trials where new regulations barring competition tyres were introduced. I bought a new pair of Dunlop Universals, being standard road-going tyres, as a result. I had worked hard on the machine beforehand trying to make sure it was absolutely sound mechanically and when I left home for the start it was motoring beautifully. The Exeter Trial is notorious for the bad weather conditions that exist at the tail end of the year and just before reaching the start, the roads became covered with ice. This was a nasty omen, I thought. For this event I had been made a travelling marshal and my job was to assist any competitor who might require it. Even-

tually I started off on the cold journey to Exeter and I had not been riding long before I saw some people waving lanterns and shouting that the road ahead was like an ice-rink. I should think that there must have been about six competitors on the ground in front of me, all having fallen off their machines on the awful surface. I dared not apply my brakes and just managed to keep aboard the Triumph, missing the fallen riders. One hazard experienced and then I had patches of fog to contend with plus a very unpleasant type of sleet. It was then that I heard my engine making a mechanical clatter which proved to be excessive clearance on the exhaust tappet which fortunately I was able to adjust by the side of the road. However, the same thing happened again and I would rather not dwell too long on the following part of my story. Repeated attempts to adjust

the tappet were experienced but things gradually grew worse until the bike just did not have sufficient power to carry me up an ordinary main road hill. I was forced to retire from that Exeter Trial without even tasting the observed sections. If only I had finished the event and failed through bad riding on the hills, I should not have felt so bad, but to fail 'like this' was heartbreaking. Of course, this sort of thing shows the type of luck which may come to any competitor in motorcycle sport. Paradoxically it turned out to be one of the easiest 'Exeters' ever and a friend of mine gained a Premier Award on this, his first long distance event. Life is a strange thing to comprehend sometimes.

Later I found that the exhaust pushrod was badly bent and really quite useless although a local garage was able to make up another rod which enabled me to get home without further trouble. But of course, the bike went like a scalded cat on that return journey.

For high speed motorcycling, I return to September 1938 when the Motorcycling Club's Brooklands meeting was to take place. I had entered my Triumph for the 2 Lap Handicap Race and one evening at our Club Headquarters I was discussing this event to come with some pals, over a glass of beer. The conversation drifted to general topics of interest and I had forgotten all about the meeting when one of our members came up to me and asked me quietly if I would care to ride his new 998cc Vincent HRD twin in place of my 350, at Brooklands. I stared at him for a moment while the significance of his offer sunk in and then, nearly spilling my beer over my trousers, I assured him that nothing could suit me better. Apparently he wanted to find out his machine's capabilities although why he should have wished to entrust me with this task had me quite baffled. However, we sat down there and then and discussed plans for the race although the only snag was that the machine would not be ready until the very day of the event and consequently I should have no chance of getting acquainted with it prior to the meeting.

We arranged to meet at the Track about an hour before the race was due to start, for any time to practise was most definitely out as I had to work on that Saturday morning and would not be able to leave the office until midday.

At last the great day arrived and we met as arranged at Brooklands. The Vincent HRD looked superb with its Brooklands silencer and racing number plates. It was only just run in and this was to be its first real test at speed. As I changed into my racing leathers the owner gave me some advice, particularly as I had not as yet ridden the machine. He said something like this 'I should take her up to 75mph in

second gear and keep in third until you are doing 90mph'. Yes, the speedometer was still on the machine. After my normal 350 bike, these figures appeared to me as quite out of this world, but I did not say so. Soon the competitors were instructed to assemble alongside the famous Vickers Sheds and, to cap everything, the Vincent's owner proudly rode the bike up to the start with me sitting on the rear pad. Imagine starting a race at Brooklands on a strange machine which you had never previously ridden. It seems almost fantastic but this was the truth of the matter. I was down to start from the scratch mark with another rider mounted on a supercharged BMW twin cylinder device. Thank goodness it was a fine day and not as the previous year's event.

After what appeared to be an age, the starter raised his flag and the first of the long line of riders screamed away towards the Home Banking. I felt nervous and fidgeted about with my goggles while attempting to keep my head clear and then quite suddenly the starter was standing by the BMW rider and myself who were now alone on the starting grid. The flag dropped and we were off at last, my nervous feeling disappearing almost at once as I let in the clutch and felt the tremendous surge of power from the big twin engine. I flattened myself on the machine's tank and to my amazement found the plot was travelling at 100mph as we reached the Home Banking. As I shot onto the Railway Straight I saw a few of the other riders spread out ahead and I managed to pass three of them before approaching the Byfleet Banking, and yet more, on flashing past the Fork.

As I started my last lap, I found that I was closing in on another bunch of riders. To me there is no sensation on earth like riding a really fast motorcycle and I felt the thrill vibrating through me as I worked onto the Home Banking again, giving thanks for my good fortune that I was riding a motorcycle with such fine handling over some of the very worst of the Brooklands bumps. Back on to the Railway Straight I attempted to squeeze myself even flatter on the Vincent HRD's tank as I passed another group of machines with the speedometer needle now showing 115mph. Then holding the bike on the Byfleet Banking, I gradually overtook yet another bunch of riders who were keeping fairly well down on this section of the track. As I passed the Fork I saw two riders ahead literally scrapping as hard as they could for the chequered flag but I failed to catch them and passed the finishing line in third place. So the race ended and I discovered that the rider of the blown BMW had won after a great ride, to be followed by a very quick Velocette whose rider had made very good use of

The super fast Vincent HRD 1000cc twin of 1938, possibly the very works model ridden by the writer at Stevenage that had impressed him so much. Post-war Vincent twins differed considerably with a wider cylinder angle one to the other, enclosed valve springs and a 'frame' that disposed of a front down tube. A far meatier Phillip Vincent designed servo action clutch was fitted, and the machine's wheelbase was shortened. The Brampton girder forks were, however, retained until the late 1940s.

Evidence of the writer's exhilarating experience at Brooklands. Note that he has added the comment 'suffering from clutch slip', being not an uncommon fault with pre-war Vincent HRD twins when given their head.

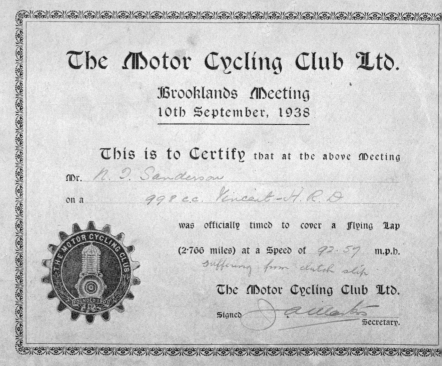

his handicap starting position. I found that the Track took a lot of learning when travelling really fast, but I had enjoyed myself tremendously and even the machine's owner was pleased. The medal I eventually received for my third place remains a much-treasured possession.

One final word—and that is that I cannot speak too highly of the superb handling of that HRD, particularly the spring frame which helped a lot. When once under way it was a total delight to ride and I have never piloted a machine that impressed me more in this respect.

Back with my Triumph 350cc Tiger I entered for a grass track meeting organized by our Club on a private field. The course was lined by tapes and any rider going outside them was automatically excluded from the race. This is precisely what happened to me when I was lying in second place, for my machine went into a slide because I opened the throttle just a little too much on a corner and I overshot the tapes. It was just bad riding on my part and I discovered that grass can be very slippery in its way and racing over it calls for a special technique which obviously I had not yet acquired. As a friend told me afterwards 'I had not got it taped'.

About this time I was fortunate enough to borrow a 350cc Ariel Red Hunter model from the dealer who originally sold me the Triumph. I entered this machine for a scramble whose course contained some of the most soul-destroying bumps for a rigid framed motorcycle to negotiate, plus a selection of sudden ascents and descents. In other words a real scrambles course. The regulations stated that the chosen plot of ground was definitely not of a frame-breaking nature, yet rather amusingly the only competitor whose frame did break was the unlucky fellow who organized the meeting and helped to word the regulations. How he had his leg pulled about this! But being a true sportsman he took it all in good part.

In the race for which I entered, six of us lined up on a very narrow path almost handlebar to handlebar. When the flag dropped the bike next to mine slid sideways and its handlebars caught me in the stomach throwing me off the Ariel. By the time I had sorted things out the others were at least half a lap in front but I tried to catch them. Very sportingly the organizers stopped this particular race to set a fresh start, but my tummy felt so painful that even with this re-run I came in last. However, the stabbing handlebar incident I could not offer as an excuse for my lowly position for I am quite sure that I could not have caught the leaders had I been much fitter.

Fortunately I was able to borrow the Red Hunter for an event held in Essex which was described as a real riders trial. There is no doubt that this was true for half the entry were stranded with water in the works at some time during the course of the trial. I took off the carburettor and cleaned it with the Ariel standing in about 18 inches of watery mud. Conditions were so bad that at one time I could not turn the twist grip throttle control because of the amount of mud on both my hands and the grip itself. From this I learnt that a rubber band cut from an old inner tube twined round the grip certainly was the answer in such circumstances. To be absolutely honest about things in this respect, I am pleased that events of this type ceased when the ban on competition tyres came into force at the end of the 1938 season. I feel that we must have been very unpopular with the general public because as we left one section, the roads were covered with mud from our machines for some distance, while the appearance of the riders plastered with the wretched stuff from head to foot cannot have been in any way a good advertisement for the sport. This is of

The Motor Cycling Club Ltd.

Brooklands Meeting
10th September, 1938

This is to Certify that at the above Meeting

Mr. R. J. Sanderson

on a 998 c.c. Vincent-H.R.D

was officially timed to cover a Flying Lap

(2·766 miles) at a Speed of 92·59 m.p.h.
suffering from clutch slip

The Motor Cycling Club Ltd.

Signed .... Secretary.

course a personal opinion, although I feel most strongly about it. By all means have a good mud plug if that is one's fancy, although to hold it on private property where the public will suffer little inconvenience appears to be so very sensible.

One final memory of that Essex trial was when a stone jammed in my rear wheel sprocket and I got off the bike which 'happily' stood up in the mud by itself.

Infinitely cleaner and certainly less demanding were club social runs, and our captain who organized one of ours decided to use an ancient Austin 7 as his particular means of transport. At one of the refreshment stops, a certain member being something of a practical joker fastened a dead rat onto the Austin's exhaust manifold and then quickly replaced the bonnet. The news of this action spread rapidly among the rest of us and when the run was resumed we rode slowly behind the captain's car in order not to miss the fun. After a mile or so the Austin's passenger was observed to be making signs and looking under the dashboard as the run continued. But a short while later the fellow could not stand things any longer and jumped from the car while at the same time holding his nose. At this spectacle we nearly fell from our machines, just shaking with laughter, and when finally the cause of such a foul odour was discovered the captain, after issuing a few choice words, accepted everything in the right spirit and jokingly vowed that he would take all kinds of reprisals on the perpetrator of the joke.

On 5th November each year the club held a wonderful Guy Fawkes party way out in the country. One of our members owned a pub there and after closing time the lads started letting off their fireworks. For the 1938 'event' it ended up with rival groups firing rockets at each other from glass bottles suitably set at an angle for the purpose. There was always a great roar from our party when we scored a direct hit on one of the rival member's plumper regions, who might be bending down at the time. I crept up behind my brother and tied a jumping cracker to his right trouser leg and, observing the directions for operating these fireworks, I lit the touch paper and retired immediately. Now my brother was much bigger than me and when the first bang went off, I had never seen such a large man move so quickly except perhaps on one occasion some years before when he was chased by a very angry bull in a Yorkshire field.

November was also the month when our annual Dinner Dance and presentation of awards won by club members during the sporting year took place. This was always a terrific evening and I am afraid that we really let our hair down on such occasions. I could not possibly attempt to write of all that went on although I clearly recall my large brother (6ft 4½in × 16st) engaged in a tango with another rather bulky male member wearing a girl's leopard-skin coat about his shoulders.

The garment had apparently been borrowed without the owner's permission and when I saw the look on the face of the coat's owner I nearly choked while attempting to maintain a straight face myself.

I mention these simple incidents because I feel that no live club can afford to be without a social side as part of its activities. On these occasions members get to know each other in a far better way than might otherwise be the case.

Just one more pleasant memory of happenings during 1938 was my visit to the Isle of Man, again for the June TT races, as spectator I hasten to add. With friends, a good viewing spot near Kate's Cottage was found where the riders can be seen all the way down to the Craig before they turn sharply to the right towards Brandish. On the day following the Junior (350cc) Race we were having some beer at the *Highlander,* being a nice pub situated by the side of the famous Course when someone mentioned that many of the racing 250cc machines left the ground at a slight bump in the road near this hostelry. One of my pals looked at me and for some reason said that the only time I would ever get my Triumph off the ground would be if I lifted it up myself. This remark rather stung me and I bet the fellow that against a pint of beer I could also get my Tiger to leave the ground over the aforementioned bump. He accepted and I went outside to my machine which was fitted with competition tyres at the time.

These items as all riders know are not really suitable for high speed motorcycling but I took the bike up the road for about a mile and then returned flat down to it. To my great pleasure the Triumph certainly left the ground for a while over that bump and eventually we all returned to the pub to enjoy his generosity of a round no less. In the early part of 1939 I became the proud owner of a Tiger 100 twin Triumph fitted with a bronze cylinder head. Although I had loved my faithful 350cc Tiger model, the smooth surge of power from the twin engine was

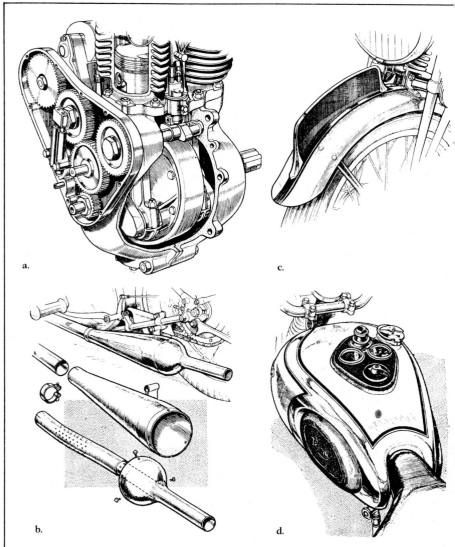

a. A sectioned view of the 1939 Tiger 100 Triumph's engine showing the revised design of cylinder base which was thicker plus an eight stud fixing of the cylinders to the crankcase. A thinner cylinder base and six studs had proved unsatisfactory on the earlier Speed Twin models. b. Standard road going silencer into racing megaphone at just a little longer than a stroke. c. The Triumph's front number plate was neatly surrounded by a chromium plated beading. d. The Tiger 100's four gallon petrol tank with quick opening filler cap, recessed knee-grips and compact instrument panel.

something which delighted my heart and I must say that in my opinion a man who has owned a fast twin cylinder bike is most unlikely to go back to a single cylinder mount again.

Soon after the Triumph was properly run in I entered it for a semi-sporting trial which more than proved to me that correctly equipped, a twin can be as successful a trials machine as a single cylinder job. The twin's slow speed pulling over a rocky section, for example, where one has to pick a path can be most helpful, although I admit that the single cylinder machine might probably have the advantage due to the slogging type power issue from its engine. I did not win an award in this trial but in fairness to the bike I must point out that I lost a first-class award only because of my bad riding in the A to B rush of a thing called a special test. On the actual sections of the trial however the twin Triumph behaved very well indeed.

For the May meeting of our annual

Speed Hill Climbs I adopted the same procedure that I had employed with my 350. I fitted an engine sprocket one tooth down from standard in order to enjoy better acceleration. I had entered for the 500cc Sports and Racing classes plus the Unlimited Sports Class and had hopes that the twin might put up a creditable performance. On my first run the speed and power of the machine nearly proved my undoing. I experienced a nasty slide just after the hairpin bend and going up towards the finish I got into a most alarming wobble which I only just managed to hold. I found that the steering damper was too slack and after this matter was given prompt attention, I had no further trouble. On my second run I was just starting to apply the brakes before the hairpin when I suddenly left the model at about 50mph. I was, however, fortunate enough to be thrown quite clear and out of the corner of my eye I saw the Tiger 100 turning somersaults on the loose sur-

face of the hill. I damaged my right leg and shoulder, but the crash helmet possibly saved my head and to this day I often will look at the dent in the helmet's crown and give thought to what could have happened *sans casque*. My brother was standing near to the scene of the crash and after one brief glance at me, he rushed to my machine and proceeded to take it slowly back to the paddock. The ambulance men on duty took me along to their mobile caravan to patch me up while my brother, although I did not know it at the time was working hard on the Triumph in an attempt to get it into reasonable shape once again. Later I discovered that the petrol tank had a hole in it, luckily near the top, and the rear brake pedal was twisted up into an amazing shape. The footrests had also suffered to a degree. Thank Heaven that apart from scratches, the machine was otherwise quite sound and when I hobbled from the caravan after a good 'repair' job by the ambul-

ance men, my brother announced that he had got the bike into a ridable state once more and that I should be able to take it in the next class for which I had entered. Personally I should not have been sorry to have called it a day, but after this remark from him I felt I just could not quit, so down we went for another shot at things.

Even now, being many years after the event, I do not really understand what caused that crash for I had four more rides up the hill after it and never experienced trouble of this nature again. Perhaps I was now travelling more slowly because I found difficulty in changing gear with my damaged leg. Eventually it was announced that I had won the 500cc Sports Class and obtained a second place in one of the other classes, thus considering every-thing I think the good twin deserved quite some praise. Although of course I did not know it then, this was to be my last shot at the Hill Climb for the Second World War broke out on the

Back in the old routine at Dancer's End, yet with a difference for 1939 events - the writer's mount now a 500cc Tiger 100 Triumph twin.

In this active shot where the model is cranked over for the latter section of the notorious hairpin bend, the offside special exhaust silencer may be seen to advantage. By removing the tail pipes, pure straight through 'mega-phones' existed which, together with the special kit of speed parts available to owners of Tiger 100s, made these Triumphs highly competitive.

very day set for our September meeting.

In 1939 there appeared in the Mo-torcycle Press an appeal from Sir Malcolm Campbell for motorcyclists with racing or trials experience to join the Territorial Army as members of a special Company under his command. I had never thought about joining the Territorials before, but this seemed just up my street if I had the necessary qualifications. I obtained my appoint-ment with Sir Malcolm who was very kind, and after asking me a few questions about my motorcycling ca-

reer, informed me that he would like to have me in his Company and would I thus report to Regent's Park Barracks for a medical test in a few days' time.

The number of men required was only about 100 and the competition was keen among volunteers who hoped to be selected. I passed the Medical and was duly enrolled as a member of the 'Bluebirds', as the Company became known. The number of my friends who had also answered the call and had been accepted was quite large, so in those immediate pre-war days it was more like a motorcycle club than an Army unit. More of this a little later.

Meanwhile as we approached the early summer, our club held a Gymkhana and in one of the events riders rode in pairs with their machines tied together with tape. The idea was that the competitors on receiving the starting signal ran to their machines, started up and raced down the field to the finish. If the tape between the machines was broken during the course of the race, the riders were then disqualified. I had teamed up with another chap riding a twin Triumph and it must be admitted that the twins are nearly always good starters so we felt we had a good chance. When the starter dropped the flag we raced for our machines and leapt into the saddles. My motor fired at once, but to our annoyance my partner's failed to respond for quite a while by which time the others were well away. When at last he got it going we did not have to worry about keeping together as we both knew we should have to ride flat out. This we did and we changed through the gears almost as one man. We just failed to catch the others but our tapes were unbroken at the finish. After the event my team mate had several shots at starting his machine, to which it responded at once on each occasion. I suppose this degree of uncertainty is what makes motorcycling, particularly competition work, such fun. Later we had a go at a spot of what was described as Balloon Bursting where riders had to manoeuvre between tapes inside which balloons had been placed at various angles. The idea was to burst each balloon with the front wheel and then race across the field to the finish where the first man to reach it after bursting every balloon was the winner. My Triumph made no mistake about destroying the balloons set in its path, and then sitting on the rear pad I raced for the finishing line. I just managed to win this event after a very exciting scrap. Simple stuff but thoroughly enjoyable!

Sir Malcolm Campbell announced that he wanted members of his Company to attend a race meeting to be held at the Crystal Palace road circuit in South London where they would ride round the course in formation display. Sir Malcolm was to lead us riding his Triumph Speed Twin model, the whole exercise being an attempt to get recruits for other motorcycle units of the Territorial Army which had been formed on similar lines to our own. No doubt the idea was sound and we were to proceed at a fairly slow pace according to the programme. I was quite near the tail of this formation and we started off in nice style, riding three abreast. Unfortunately or fortunately if you may subscribe to my point of view, the leaders started to ride more quickly than was originally planned, with the result that we were batting round at quite a fair speed towards the finish and it nearly developed into a private scrap. Needless to say we all enjoyed this and I heard later that it did bring in recruits, so the story had a happy ending after all.

I had been having some trouble with the hardened end caps of the pushrods on my Tiger 100. These tended to break and I could not put the matter right myself so I wrote to Triumphs and told them about it. They wrote back and asked me if I would ride the machine to their Coventry works, which I promptly did. The boss of the Competitions Department suggested that I took myself off to a cinema and call back in about three hours or so. Taking his advice, I went off to see a couple of good films and three hours later I returned to Triumphs to find that they had completely stripped the engine down, replaced the pushrods and now the bike was ready for me to ride back home and no charge to me at all. I thought this to be a very kind action and the trouble was well and truly cured.

With the Triumph all well and good, once again I entered it for a Brooklands meeting organized by 'our' Sir Malcolm Campbell. The event was for members of his Bluebirds Company and was to be run over the truer road-racing Campbell circuit. For this meeting which was staged on the handicap basis I recall that my entry fee was one

shilling and sixpence, and Sir Malcolm had arranged for a first prize of £15 to be given to the winner and smaller cash awards to the next three finishers. There were about five Tiger 100s on the entry list, but some of the 350cc machines had a 1 minute 20 seconds start over we 500cc people. One of the 350s was a pukka Manx Norton, incidentally. At the starter's signal off we went, and I was fortunate enough to be first away among the twins, and in fact none of them passed me during the race. Racing on that Campbell circuit was very interesting from the rider's point of view. From the start, which was situated on a straight stretch of road, competitors took a sharp right-hand bend and then dropped down to where the Course swept up to the left onto the famous Home Banking. The rider then went along the Railway Straight for some distance before turning sharp left onto the road circuit again. After a few right and left bends he was faced with a sweeping left hander, which had a very nasty bump on it, bringing the front wheels very much off the ground before the

rider approached the straight past the start once again. During the race, as my twin reached the Railway Straight on each lap, I saw one of the fast 350s just making the left turn some way ahead. I could not help thinking what a wonderful scrap I should have had with that 350 if the 1 minute 20 seconds difference in our starting-time had been cancelled. I thoroughly enjoyed the race, particularly the part where I had to negotiate the sweeping left-hand bend to which I have already made reference. At this point I was able to take it flat out in third gear at about 90mph. I eventually finished in fifth place, just missing some beer money.

And so to August 1939 when our Company, under Sir Malcolm's command, went to a Territorial Camp where we were trained to be soldiers in the real sense of the word. Some of us were allowed to take our own motorcycles with us and we were paid 10 shillings per day for this which, at the time, I considered quite good. We were under canvas and were nearly washed away several times by the foul

Of Sergeant Major sayings: 'You might break your mother's heart but you will never break mine'. Lance Corporal Norman Sanderson on 'uke', Burley Territorial Army Camp, 1939.

wet weather of that time. The Sergeant Major tried his best to break our hearts and yet, at the end of our stay, we clubbed together and bought him a present. What a strange world we live in! I cannot say that I enjoyed this camp but we had plenty of fun at times, while the general experience was soon to prove most useful with war so imminent.

Here my story ends, for it is not my intention to write of major conflict between nations for we know quite enough about that. It is, however, my hope that some of the experiences that were mine in those on the whole, sweet pre-war years, may have proved of interest, where I enjoyed to the full one of the finest pastimes going . . . motorcycling.

LIGHTWEIGHT SIDECAR

The days of the big old slogger and sidecar are gone and if you want such a bike today, at a practicable price, you must aim at a lighter machine. DENNIS HOWARD has been to see what became of today's few appropriate machines, an MZ, when it underwent the sidecar treatment.

One can immediately dismiss the ancient comment that no motorcycle under 500cc should be used for sidecar work, although this was true to some degree a few years ago. Modern low capacity motorcycles are quite capable of hauling efficiently a suitable sidecar providing, of course, that they possess a well-designed and sufficiently robust frame and fork assembly, plus a power unit having a good low-down pulling ability. In other words it is a matter of selecting the right tool for the job. Keeping things in proportion is, however, necessary and it is suggested that one should not burst into a state of rash enthusiasm and attach a sidecar to just any machine of under 250cc unless one can claim to be an expert in this rather specialized field. For gen-

The moment of departure from Hampstead: owner John Bray is at the controls of his 1976 TS Model MZ while the writer occupies the passenger position.

The simple and very functional Briggs designed sidecar chassis with three connection points. Tubing is 10 gauge by 1½in mild steel.

All is revealed in the Harry Briggs workshops. In the absence of a front down tube on the TS range of 250 MZs, the forward sidecar connection is attached to a substantial clamp fitted on the machine's two large diameter tubes that form the basis of the MZ's spine frame. Eventually the writer was able to persuade the bike's owner to discard that awful top box assembly.

eral purposes a quarter litre outfit is about the smallest to which one should consider going.

Of the right type of 250 machine available today, perhaps the East German MZ is the best willing workhorse in the making of a nippy lightweight sidecar outfit, the Zschopau-built two stroke (formerly DKW and largest manufacturers of motorcycles throughout the world up to 1939) is fashioned by sufficiently down-to-earth folk who continue to ensure that their products remain simply and seriously efficient vehicles of transport rather than devices played on the gimmicky theme.

Sadly, the United Kingdom concessionaires for MZ machines ceased some years ago to import the superb little 250cc sidecar outfits, although Redditch-based Harry Briggs, sometime-titled 'Sidecar King of the Midlands', produces an excellent quality no-nonsense lightweight sidecar to complement the TS series 250 MZ range of motorcycles. In this knowledge an MZ-owning friend and myself recently took *Lizzie,* heroine of a five-month 12,500-mile journey through Europe, to be mated—if I may use such an expression—to a Briggs standard model lightweight sports sidecar.

It is a strange experience to leave one's home base on a sprightly solo machine and to return some hours later with a device that requires to be driven rather than ridden in the accepted sense, any stylish weaving and leaning becoming all so quickly something of the past. There are even moments, if one possesses a certain sentimental turn of mind, of sadness that the once free-as-a-bird solo might well be shackled to its new companion for the rest of its working life. Any blues in this direction soon pass quite rapidly, however, for the MZ is built for sidecar use if necessary and indeed might well be never happier than when it is. There is an old saying in motorcycling circles 'once a sidecar man always a sidecar man', for such is the unique attraction of handling a well set up outfit and in no lesser consideration does there exist the immense practical uses to which a bike and chair may be put.

A well set up outfit, the very key to sidecar driving enjoyment and unless one fully understands the certain science of sidecar fitting, possesses suitable facilities plus a perfectly level

Further attachment points are made with a Briggs clamp assembly on the MZ's seat rail and on the pillion footrest arm. The sidecar connection for the former has yet to be swung up and bolted to the lug [just slightly forward of the suspension unit top]. Adjustment here is made for the degree that the motorcycle must lean away from the sidecar. At this period during the mating process, the sidecar wheel has already been given its degree of 'toe in'.

Set by the manufacturer during the sidecar chassis construction period, 'lead', that is, the distance that the sidecar wheel is situated forward of the rear wheel of the motorcycle, is 8in.

Never a dull moment at the Briggs Redditch-based works. Here, Harry's eldest son Roger works on a lightweight sports model sidecar body.

workshop floor, one is urged not to have a go along the DIY line but to leave it to the expert who really knows what he is doing and will naturally make a professional job of things.

Harry Briggs is an expert, having had years of experience in the game. His workshops are part of many neat new buildings on an industrial estate situated between Redditch and Studley and it is here that *Lizzie* came for the attaching of that 'third wheel' and all that goes with it.

For the uninitiated, I should explain that the TS series MZ has no front down tube and as such an item has most times been the very anchor upon which a front sidecar connection has depended, I was eager to know how Harry Briggs got round the problem! I suppose one might say that it is easy when one knows how, for with the MZ's petrol tank removed and the two large diameter tubes that form the very basis of its spine frame in evidence, a very substantial split clamp was attached a short distance down from the steering head upon these tubes. On the other hand, where the MZ factory include a suitable sidecar attachment tube lug just beneath the saddle nose section of the frame, this is not used, as Harry prefers to fit a further horizontally positioned clamp across the seat rails much further rearward, plus another attachment point utilizing the nearside pillion footrest lug. Presumably the thinking here is that it is better to spread the attachment point distances for greater rigidity as a whole. Incidentally, all final tightening of clamps, etc, comes when the setting up process is completed and last checks have been made.

Now comes the scientific part of the operation where the sidecar chassis is offered up to the MZ. A suitable length of straight wood is placed alongside the wheels of the motorcycle to check and, to a degree, maintain the wheels remaining in line while another is ready to be put against the chassis wheel when the connections between MZ and chassis are loosely bolted up. At this time the two lengths of wood

Final adjustments are made to the MZ and its newly acquired sidecar chassis before the body, waiting patiently over on the far left, will be fitted. Characters are, from left to right: the writer, silver locked Harry Briggs [64], who always has a salty tale to tell, and then visitor to the works on this occasion, ex-Grand Prix Lago Talbot driver Peter Waring. The MZ's owner, John Bray, stands close to the door. Bending over the machine is Roger Briggs.

Hey presto! For after a few hours in the Briggs workshops a really fascinating little sidecar outfit emerges. The sidecar's hood and side curtains are stowed away, when not required behind the seat rest. Hood is supported in the up position by a removable steel hoop slotted into suitable points on inner section of sidecar body.

will run parallel to each other. However, it is essential that the chassis wheel will be given what is referred to as a degree of 'toe in', meaning that this wheel must not, in fact, run parallel to the wheels of the motorcycle but turn in slightly towards the machine so that when the outfit is

being ridden, the wheel 'presses' against the latter. This adjustment in the Briggs fitting for lightweight sidecars is about ½in and is made by pulling the sidecar chassis over towards the front end of the MZ. It will now be understood why the two lengths of wood from which the correct measurements are taken will no longer remain parallel but be 'cut' by half an inch. This setting of 'toe in' and its correct adjustment ensures the automatic straightforward run of the outfit on a level road.

Equally as important as 'toe in' is the degree to which the motorcycle leans away from the sidecar, being a requirement to compensate for the curvature of the road surface and the slight scraping of the sidecar tyre involved by the 'toe'. Again adjustments are made at the sidecar connection clamps although Harry Briggs does not necessarily consider any specific measurement here being necessary but prefers to attend to this 'by eye' so that when one is looking at the assembled motorcycle and chassis

from front to rear, the motorcycle is 'just off the vertical' and no more. However, with such adjustments it is often necessary to take into account how often a sidecar passenger is to be carried and, to a degree, the weight of such a being.

Lastly comes the question of 'lead', being the distance that the sidecar wheel is situated forward of the rear wheel of the motorcycle. Too great a lead will require more muscular effort on the part of the outfit's driver when putting the device through curves, and increased wear and tear on tyres, whereas too small a lead increases the danger of tilting the outfit over, particularly when curves are taken at high speeds. Thus sidecar manufacturers work on the happy medium principle and usually fix a suitable lead, which is set when the actual sidecar chassis is constructed, taking into consideration, of course, the type or model of motorcycle to which the sidecar is to be attached. For the 250 MZ fitted with a Briggs lightweight sidecar, the lead measurement is just 8 inches.

Making ready for the return run to London: the writer had whizzed the outfit around the block and reported 'all systems satisfactory'. Note the lean-out angle of motorcycle to sidecar. With a heavy passenger, lean will be reduced to some degree as sidecar sinks on the chassis wheel suspension unit. Adjustments must be made according to type of going envisaged.

At this point it may be appreciated that only when a sidecar is properly fitted to a motorcycle will the outfit handle correctly and why the well-meaning type who is of the opinion that one merely sticks a sidecar to the steed will never experience the sheer joy of driving such a device and may well ruin the frame, wheels, tyres and many other parts of his machine as a result.

A point raised with Harry was the matter of fork rake, or trail as it is sometimes called. This is all to do with front fork angle set against the steering head and determines wheel-base length and so on. Some years ago when the majority of motorcycles were fitted with girder pattern forks, it was necessary if going over from solo to sidecar to increase the fork rake and, in so doing, increase the wheelbase by substituting shorter top fork links. If one neglected to do this, the front wheel would possess a marked tendency to engage in an alarming degree of patter from one side to another, particularly when one was driving the outfit at slow speeds or throttling off. In a modern setting, leading link or triangulated pattern front forks specifically designed for sidecar use are by far the best although, without major surgery, I could see no way in which the telescopic forks as fitted to *Lizzie* could be changed to provide 'sidecar trail'. However, HB advises that as long as one screws the steering damper well and truly down, one need not concern oneself unduly about front wheel patter during sidecar use.

Once a final check is made to ensure that all adjustments are correct, the nut and bolt tightening process is completed at all connections and the chassis is ready to receive the sidecar body, or boat as it was once called. A nice little affair is this body with its simple four point attachment where bolts pass through the sidecar floor to easily located lugs situated on the chassis 'square'.

So to a test just around the block and everything appears well, and there is some relief that *Lizzie*'s owner remembered to lower the MZ's gearing by fitting a smaller gearbox sprocket . . . very important to attend to this . . . very! The 108-mile journey back to London was just fine as the little outfit was swung through the A34 and later the A40's many bends. Power on through the left handers to keep the sidecar wheel on the deck while a touch of front brake on right handers to bring the sidecar round so nicely— a sidecar well fitted and a joy to drive!

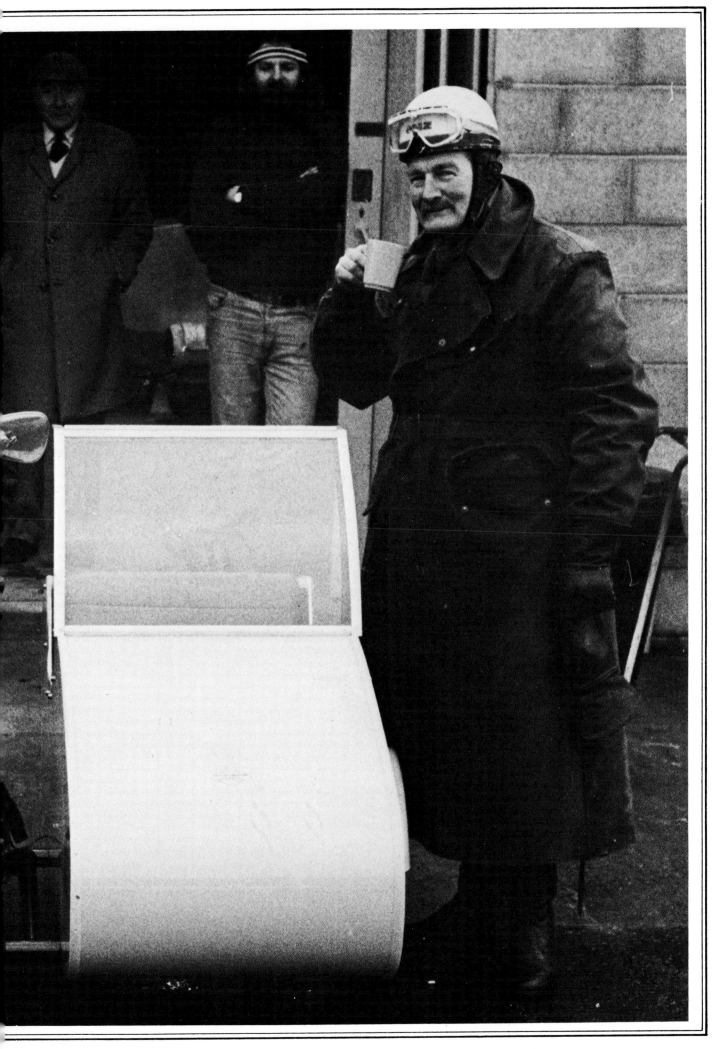

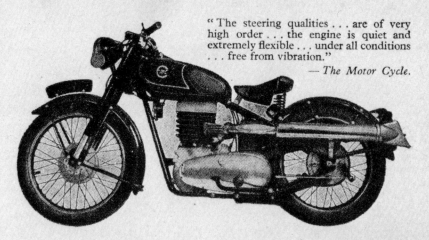
CAME BUT NEVER CONQUERED

A brand new British motorcycle in 1947 created a deep impression on DENNIS HOWARD which has stayed with him for more than thirty years. All-but forgotten today, the story of the EMC has been meticulously pieced together by Dennis to record an exciting project that sadly went awry.

In the spring of 1947 the writer had wandered down the warm pavements of Watford High Street towards a little shop called Englands to view the latest motorcycle stock and where three examples of thoroughbred category unused pre-war machines existed on show. Such was the pleasure afforded any caller to look upon these beauties in forms D Special Levis, Rudge Ulster and Excelsior Manxman, all possessing the slightly bloomed appearance that marks the classic breed, that the proprietor had decided, quite sensibly, that they should not be sold.

Now over thirty years on and with the friendly little shop long gone, one

wonders just what became of that lovely trio. If, God willing, they still exist, one hopes that they are far away from the hands of 'prestige people'!

Undoubtedly a great attraction, the noble oldsters were obliged, however, to occupy a rearward place in the small showroom while a veritable upstart of a thing looking, in those days, big, black and rather awesome, more than ably hogged the window for all to see. Exciting? . . . yes, for here stood an entirely new British motorcycle with no question of a pre-war rehash. Although a two-stroke, this was not so very obvious at first viewing, for the machine had a massive rough cast

A 1948 EMC advertisement, its wording suggesting the undoubted advantages of owning a machine with such petrol-consuming efficiency, particularly during a period when fuel was still rationed.

Operating details of the 350cc 'split single' EMC engine showing how differential port timing was possible. In the left-hand drawing, the pistons are shown in their descending sequence while the right-hand drawing shows them in ascent.

The vertical arrow indicates transfer passage of fresh mixture from crankcase to combustion chamber and horizontal arrows for inlet and exhaust. The inlet port is uncovered as the right hand piston approaches top dead centre.

Cast iron cylinder block with three ports in forward 'transfer' cylinder, while rear cylinder has three exhaust ports and two inlet. Bore 50mm and stroke 88mm. Aluminium head of 'penthouse' shape internally with sparking plug situated above transfer cylinder area. Compression ratio 6.6 to 1. Specialloid aluminium alloy pistons with exhaust/inlet item 111mm in length and transfer piston 99mm. Each piston fitted with three compression rings and three circumferential oil grooves set at equal distances between lower ring and gudgeon pin boss. Bottom 'collecting' groove feeds oil to gudgeon pin through piston boss. Both 16mm diameter gudgeon pins plus wrist pin of slave connecting rod of hardened steel although small end eyes and lower eye of slave rod of non-hardened material. Theory here that hard and soft steels provide a good bearing surface. Steel flywheel assembly running in single ball races and $1\frac{3}{16}$ inch diameter crankpin press fitted into flywheels. Caged rollers $\frac{1}{2} \times \frac{1}{4}$ inch for big end assembly. Crankcase compression seals consist of two ·020 inch spring steel shims with $\frac{1}{8}$ inch steel spacer ring in each side of engine kept in contact with main bearings by mainshaft nuts having ground inner faces.

oblong cylinder block, high as high can be, suggesting that conveniently hidden away in tunnels beneath the very substantial cooling fins might well exist all the necessary odds and ends to play a four stroke tune. Strangely enough, although this 350 conceived by Josef Ehrlich was most certainly a two stroke that was 'different', its exhaust note was very similar to that of a four stroke, which had countless enthusiasts and non-enthusiasts alike stressing the point on every possible occasion.

Some two stroke! for contrary to the usually accepted petrol-thirsty shortcomings of an otherwise attractive principle where fewer moving parts are in motion compared with a four stroke, Joe's EMC (Ehrlich Motor Company) could apparently be mean on fuel consumption even if subjected to what we may describe as a moment or two's pressing on speeds. It was all a matter of an efficient well-thought-out system, according to the maker, who laid great emphasis on this important detail, particularly as at this period petrol rationing still existed.

To suggest that Ehrlich had evolved a totally new system in advanced two-stroke design would be wrong, for

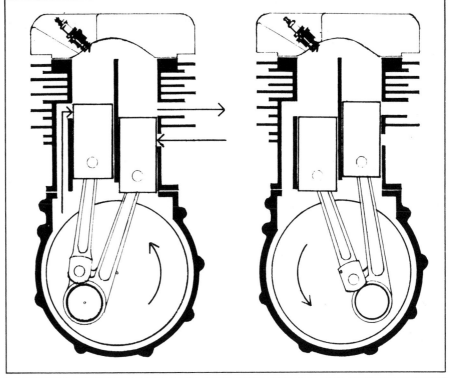

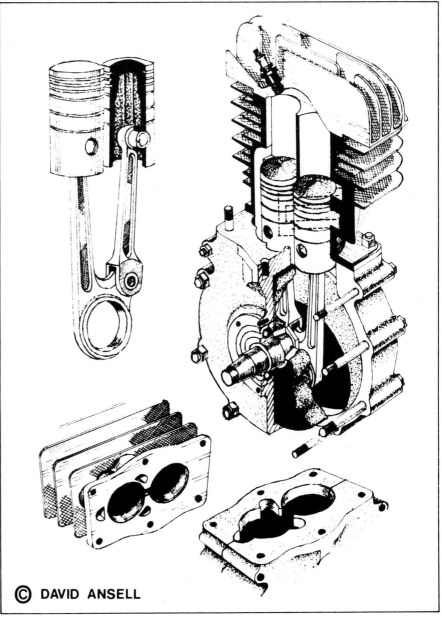

© DAVID ANSELL

Trim and advanced in concept, this racing 350 EMC of 1948/1949 contravened the post-war regulations governing types of engine permitted. The machine had a crankcase mounted phasing piston working inside the cylinder, seen here beneath the radiator of the water cooling system. Of a double acting type, the piston could assist crankcase depression and compression periods during the two stroke cycle of operations. If not supercharging, then something coming quite near to such. Following normal EMC design in its working split single, cylinder arrangement, the power unit it was claimed, developed 45bhp. A Mr White of Baltimore offered £5,000 for this 'banned' racer.

Really a very different EMC story. Hans Burman wheels his 125cc Puch engined model during a break in practice for the 1952 Ultra-Lightweight TT. Burman finished in sixth place in the actual race. A number of production models were made for the private owner and proved quite successful. The writer witnessed his first EMC/Puch at Crystal Palace about 1954 and remembers it being very noisy.

---

more was it a case of an already tried and proved method pioneered by the Austrian Puch, DKW and TWN (German Triumph) concerns some years before the war, now suitably reworked and, to a degree, refined by Joe. However, the EMC was 100% a British made motorcycle, right down to the valve cores of its (most times) fitted Dunlop—as opposed to other manufacturers—inner tubes. As with Puch and TWN road-going motorcycles, the EMC engine was of the split or double single two-stroke type in which two pistons operating in their respective cylinders were served by a combustion chamber common to both.

Where Puch and TWN employed a truly forked connecting rod, the actual parting of the ways being about half-way up from the crankpin assembly, plus in some cases, a special system of sliding small end eye and rectangular gudgeon pin to accept the variation in gudgeon pin centres during each revolution of the flywheels, the EMC used a master connecting rod on which a suitable joint existed about its big end eye to carry a slightly smaller 'slave' rod. However, in all designs the basic principle of operation was much the same. On the DKW, such things as articulated connecting rods, twin pistons and so on were restricted to the ultra-sophisticated race machines where fuel economy was a minor consideration, when great power and speed were the prime requisites.

Looking at the split single design simply it was an actual 'dividing' of the operations in the two stroke cycle so that one cylinder took care of transfer duties while the other dealt with inlet and exhaust phases, each cylinder having its appropriately situated port areas. By reason of the piston dwell that existed in this type of engine, the exhaust ports could open and close a fraction earlier than the transfer outlets, giving a port timing certainly not possible with the conventional 'single bore' three port two stroke. On the latter, an incurable fault was that a good volume of fresh charge could not be prevented from passing out in an unburnt state with the exhaust gases from the engine's 'just passed' firing moment. As the piston descended and opened the exhaust port, it also uncovered the transfer outlet, permitting a scavenging operation (use of incoming charge to assist in pushing out spent gases) of very doubtful efficiency.

What of the man Joe Ehrlich, he who was playing a familiar tune on a different instrument—his instrument, the EMC? An Austrian by birth, Joe had at one time raced the odd motorcycle here and there in his native country but by 1939 when he had settled in England, his first Ehrlich engined motorcycle, albeit strictly experimental, was demonstrated at Brooklands. Later, during the war years, the young designer, still in his twenties, had hoped to interest the War Office in a proposed military version of his dual piston two stroke creation, smartly slipping a suitable unit into a spare Ariel frame for evaluation by the appropriate brass of the day. However, as the war was now at the fag-end stage of its more desperate intensity and already much slackening of neckties was taking place, new military motorcycle designs were, for the time being at least, not required! If the current crop of war buffs might intend to reposition Heaven and Earth in the pursuit of owning a military motorcycle, the situation in 1946 was anything but, with the gallant Jack Service back in civvy street calling out for the black enamel and chromium-plated jobs of Britain's peacetime programme. What better opportunity was there for Ehrlich to try his luck!

If much different in concept to the traditional meal of four stroke single that marked *the* British motorcycle in pre-war days and was expected again by the oh, so very conservative rider, the EMC, although appealing thus to a limited motorcycling public, was a fascinating thing. Consider, however, that thirty-five years ago the two stroke was the exception rather than the rule and even if a tough little camp of two stroke diehards existed, the four stroke and its followers still ruled the day, and indeed were to do so for some years to come.

With this known quantity did Joe Ehrlich have a problem? Apparently not, according to J. E.'s reckoning, for his design of two stroke, although just a little more complicated in its works department, spelt efficiency—and how!—with a claimed 100 miles of going given in exchange for one precious gallon of petrol—not an unattractive feature for any 350cc motorcycle, be it two or four stroke.

Could it just be that, with the impressive title of Ehrlich Motor Company, one might have conjured up comfortable thoughts of a business of substantial proportion set in an industrially romantic part of Birmingham, the very cradle of British motorcycle manufacture? Not so, for the factory, consisting of several prefabricated type sheds, was in a typical spot of London suburbia at Twyford Abbey Road, Park Royal, NW10, just a short distance from the point where the North Circular Road and Western Avenue embrace. Later a move was made to new premises at St Mary's Works, Southall Lane, Southall, Middlesex.

Built by a working crew of about sixteen to twenty, the Mk I EMC was ready for human consumption in April 1947 and the writer must assume that the model seen in Englands' (how appropriate!) window was one of the very first deliveries to local agents. Other than the obviously interesting power unit, the EMC was quite conventional in general specification and during its early days of manufacture, about two per week if the wind were in the right direction, could be described as an assembly job, where proprietary fittings, being the products of other manufacturers, are used to form a motorcycle as a whole.

To their credit, EMC were the first off the mark to fit Dowty telescopic front forks to their machines. In dimension not much thicker than a solid pair of working broomsticks, these forks were air sprung and oil damped, their only regular attention being the necessity of applying a normal tyre pump to a Schrader valve positioned on the top end of one leg whenever natural deflation had taken place above a specified degree. Red dots on the lower sliders were indicators by their position in relation to the fork shrouds as to when a spot of pumping might be necessary. Linked by a connecting pipe, air introduced to one leg automatically attended to the other, and being sensitive in their way to differing weights carried, a harder measure of 'springing' was recommended when a pillion passenger might be taken.

Attractive to the writer on seeing his first EMC in Spring (*ack* Frederick Delius) was its neat twin tube frame, the tubes running from a very businesslike manganese bronze casting that formed not only the steering head but the frame backbone all in one. Passing *cleanly* under the machine's crankcase and gearbox sections, the tubes continued on their way to terminate at the rear wheel spindle area.

Should the modern reader question the reason for the writer's brief moment of joy, experienced when looking at the smooth lines of that duplex frame, it might be explained that this was a time when the typically British motorcycle still possessed a stout di-

ameter single tube running from steering head to frame cradle. Thus, twin
down tubes were an advanced feature
of motorcycle frame design and appreciated by those who cared. However,
for all the immediate pleasure inspecting a nice neat frame by courtesy of
the Ehrlich Motor Company, it was
later learned on good authority that
these structures were surplus to re-
quirements from the pre-war SOS
concern, purveyors of jolly, water-

cooled two strokes to that tough little
camp of enthusiasts mentioned earlier
in the story. For the uninitiated the
letters SOS meant Super Onslow Special, origin Birmingham, the makers
being early experimenters with twin
tube, welded frames.

The special steering head-*cum*-back-
bone assembly, an aluminium casting
on later EMC models, was, to the
writer's knowledge, no part of SOS
frame production, however.

Whether or not Joe Ehrlich had
visions of an EMC empire with his
special type of two stroke becoming a
vital part of the British motorcycling
scene, given time, of course, is not
known. However, contemporary sales
literature gave more than a suggestion
that the EMC would appeal most
certainly to the rider who demanded
quality of workmanship and efficiency
of product. Regardless of the very best
proprietary fittings supplied by leading

seats, etc. Sadly not a success, the spring heel frame project was abandoned although it is known that several such frames were exported to Australia and Sweden, countries that over the EMC's production years 1947 to 1952, when 1500 machines were made, received more than two-thirds of the firm's total output. However, by the time the Ehrlich Motor Company folded in 1952 no major changes of any real significance had taken place in EMC design or manufacture.

Oh, what a pity that the EMC was never a winner as a roadgoing motorcycle. Paradoxically, it enjoyed a small measure of success when rigged out as an out-and-out racing device and here it is necessary to stress that the models so used were pure Ehrlich engined bikes and not those of another house racing under the EMC banner during the same period. Come to 1954 and journey onwards to the late 1960s to yet a different story of very considerable glory for mighty rapid racing 125cc machines carrying the distinctive EMC decal on their tanksides.

There is a saying that if a thing looks right then it surely is right. Was Joe Ehrlich's original 350 so wrong in concept and presentation that never would it shine? In the writer's opinion the basically sound principles of the EMC two stroke system, plus the admittedly unusual but certainly not unattractive appearance of the machine as a whole, should have earned it a better place in the motorcycle ratings. For sure the EMC would never have won over the dedicated four stroke types from their hallowed dens, but with time on his side, the day of the Japanese disc and reed valve two strokes yet to dawn for a vast motorcycling public, one might have hoped that Joe Ehrlich would eradicate the odd faults in his design and come bouncing back into the market-place.

The original Scotts were not so hot, so Alfred applied 'operation rethink'. It worked, as the special people are only too aware.

Elsewhere in this book are accounts of EMCs on test and in International Six Days Trials going.

British manufacturers, the EMC just did not sell even on that score. Efficiency? No, other than the machine's ability to provide a very low tickover speed and a marked lack of 'four stroking' when running light, given but a moderate twist of the throttle when under way, never would it give anything near the claimed magic 100 miles to the gallon. On the contrary, it was ever a thirsty beast, justly 'appreciated' by its pilot when taken to the limit of just over seventy miles per hour, and in addition it vibrated unpleasantly at such a speed.

Pressing on and apparently undeterred by the many unfavourable comments coming from dissatisfied owners, and dealers who found it the hardest task to shift an EMC from their showrooms, Joe Ehrlich was offering plunger spring heels on his 1948 models and other niceties in the way of conical wheel hubs and dual

LOW SPEED THRILLS
and Hilarity

The very essence of motorcycle sport was distilled at Crystal Palace in the far-off late Twenties when intrepid 'Trade' and 'Private' enthusiasts took to their mounts for those gripping 'Path Races'. GUY ASHENDEN was on the spot fifty years ago and looks back on them now with great affection.

Guy Ashenden became infected by the motorcycling bug at the age of ten when two masters at his prep school, one possessing a two stroke 'Baby' Triumph and the other a Zenith 'Super Eight' outfit, would take him to 'away' cricket matches on or in their respective machines. When a pupil at Bed-

ford Modern School, Mr Ashenden's French master, Raoul de Choisey, continued the outings for this youngster, taking him pike fishing on the pillion of his four valve Ricardo Triumph and later in the passenger seat of a sports Aero Morgan-Anzani.

The author has described a period

of five utterly miserable years as a servant of Martins Bank, Bromley, between 1926 and 1931, although in 1928 Mr Ashenden acquired his first motorcycle, a 1924 344cc Zenith-JAP.

Joining the West Kent MCC, and then the Sidcup & District Club in 1933, 'Ash' engaged in quite a bit of

'This is not to say that the "charioteers" never struck trouble, they most certainly did'. W. H. Friend tips his Scott outfit during an event at The Palace in the early 1930s.

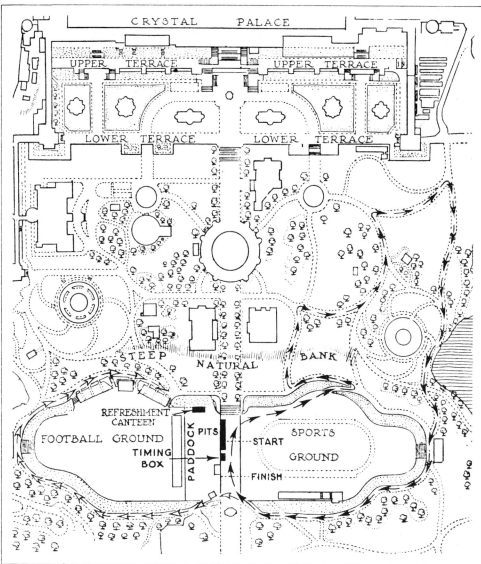

The original Crystal Palace path racing course indicated by the dark arrows.

'entirely unspectacular grass track and sprint hill climbing activity', even to covering a few laps at Brooklands before a front tyre ran off its rim, causing the rider to crash at about 80 mph. Returning to a time of equal misery where banking had been replaced by work for an insurance company, Guy Ashenden eventually moved to Cambridgeshire where, as an assistant to a most unpleasant salesman of Shepreth Motors from 1934 to 1936, the author recalls an occasion thus: 'I finally had to knock the b...... out cold and take £10 he owed me for my profit on a number of tyres I had sold . . . this was on the day I left and I removed the cash from the blighter's till while he lay on the floor beside his desk . . . after this his chief mechanic jumped onto the pillion of my AJS and insisted that I take him to a pub at Melbourn in order that he could buy me a beer in gratitude for my spectacular action'.

In 1936 the author became fascinated by aviation matters and studied for a flight radio officer's licence at Waddon Road School, Croydon, where, during his period of study, he was employed by Marconi's [Aircraft] Section at Croydon Airport. Passing successfully in June 1938, the author then took his private pilot's licence on a Gipsy Moth at Redhill Flying Club.

As a freelance FR/O for various firms in Croydon until October 1938, Mr Ashenden moved on to Wrightways Air Services, flying English newspapers to Paris on a seven days per week roster system, operations being so organized that the papers would be on sale in Paris by 8a.m. Here DH Rapides and 86s were used.

The author joined the RAF just after the outbreak of World War II but was eventually released on account of his AM FR/O's licence and flew as a civilian radio officer with RAF Ferry Command from 1941 to 1945. While serving in Canada, Mr Ashenden owned a 1938 Model 18 Norton and a 1939 Ariel Square Four and, joining the Montreal Sports MCC, did much long distance touring in the Laurentian Mountain district on both machines. Mr Ashenden remains a dedicated motorcyclist to this day and owns a very sporting 350cc Blackburne engined Henley of 1924/6 vintage. The author raced this machine at Silverstone in 1950 while more recently the splendid device has taken part in several Mallory Park and Brands Hatch parades as well as a succession of Banbury Runs organized by the Vintage Motorcycle Club. It is also used for daily transport.

*   *   *

'Really, Joyce, it is plucky of you to come here on such a beastly day!' 'My dear—I wouldn't miss it for the worlds!'

And how VERY right she was!

Now this bit of conversation between two attractive young girls took place on a raw, miserable November afternoon in the grounds of Crystal Palace over fifty years ago. The reason for it? Motorcycle racing. In a copy of *The Motor Cycle* in May 1927 appeared the headline: 'Road Racing Comes to London'.

Well, as I suppose the late 'Professor' C. E. M. Joad might have commented, 'It all depends on what you mean by "a road".'

Chasing Velocette No 76 is Norton-mounted Eric Thompson during the course of the 6th August meeting in 1927. A Crystal Palace 'regular' in those days, Eric later went on to serve the Vintage Motor Cycle Club very honourably as its National Secretary.

With one mile to the lap, the course wound and twisted like a snake in torment; at least eight-tenths of it was no more than 15ft wide, while most of the surface was very loose indeed. In later years it was more accurately described as 'path racing', for one can well visualize nursemaids wheeling babies round the circuit in their prams on sunny mornings. When I add that the penultimate lap record up to the final closure of the circuit in 1934 was made by that immortal road racing 'ace', the late Harold Daniell on his 490cc Norton at a shade under 33 mph, one can get a pretty good idea of just how tricky it was.

Freddie Mockford and Cecil Smith of *London Motor Sports* started it all, and for doing so they must have earned the everlasting gratitude of many thousands of fanatically enthusiastic competitors and spectators together, for crowds of around 15,000 were quite normal at meetings held on Saturday afternoons and midweek evenings from May to November under the Mockford/Smith management. Between 1933 and 1934 the Streatham MCC took over as organizers.

Races were divided into two 'classes'—'Trade' and 'Private Owner' and were the days, of course, when only the trade riders took their machines to a meeting stripped and ready for immediate action, carried usually on a sidecar float. On the other hand, the private owner had one motorcycle and rode to work on it every day, took his popsie to the flicks or the palais de danse on the pillion on Saturday night, went away for his annual holiday on it, and used it to compete in a trial or on the local grass track at weekends. Naturally, if he decided to 'have a bash' at the Crystal Palace racing he rode it there, standard pump petrol in the tank, silencer[s], lighting set [usually 'stink lamps'—i.e., acetylene gas operated], with his crash hat slung at the end of one handlebar—or strapped to his belt—and a bag of tools over his shoulder. Upon arrival at the start he removed silencer and lights, donned helmet, and was all set to go! Clothing was informal in the extreme: cord breeches, 'up to the knee' woollen stockings and shoes were frequently seen, and more than one rider competed with his shirt sleeves rolled up in hot weather, despite horrendous clouds of dust that were raised about the circuit. Goggles seemed to be the exception rather than the rule—they did tend to steam up quite readily—probably due to the moderate speeds

and the resultant lack of 'quick' cold air against the safety glass.

The starting area opposite the timing box was, if my memory is not too widely at fault, about 25–30 yards wide, and only about 40 yards after the starting line competitors turned fairly sharp right into a positive bottle-neck, being entry to a 15ft wide winding slight incline leading to the famous Maze Hairpin. There followed a very tight left hander, then round a left curve for about 120 yards to Three Tree Corner, right again, followed by a very narrow twisting section to Statue Hairpin, again right, and wind on to Rockhills Hairpin, very sharp right leading to The Lake Stretch, winding downhill with thick bushes each side, the lake on the left, under overhanging tree boughs, to a bridge with a nasty concrete affair at each corner. Survive this, and one peeled into the Stand Stretch [at rear of a grandstand erected, I believe, for spectating at a small out-of-use banked cycle race track] and probably the fastest part of the circuit. Once past the stand one took a right-hand dive down onto the starting area to commence the next lap.

Owing to the nature of the course, races were divided into heats, two riders per heat, starting at 15-second intervals, while sidecar entries were started singly at similar intervals.

Riders in each heat were provided with coloured singlets—white stripes round a black singlet, red on white, green on yellow, etc, etc., also whole colours: red, blue, green and so on. The colour of singlet plus the individual rider's numbers were noted in the programme, thus. Despite the time-interval starting method, the fact that the circuit measured a mere one mile per lap, at least two-thirds of which could be seen from any one viewpoint, the racing was infinitely easier to follow than was the case in the Isle of Man TT or Manx GP with its 37¾ mile lap, ridden seven times round. Towards the end of a typical TT, a spectator was usually completely fogged as to the placings of the riders, unless seated in the grandstand opposite the vast scoreboard, in which case where riding ability was to be studied one might as well be at a quarter-mile sprint meeting.

However, this path racing at Crystal Palace WAS thrilling; the under 30 mph lap speeds did not detract from the excitement in the very least and, as nearly all bikes had three speed gearboxes in those days, I doubt if many of 500cc ever used top gear, the exceptions possibly being those of the 'trade' riders who probably had very close ratio gears fitted and small engine sprockets.

The spectators provided much of the entertainment, rushing like a herd of frightened sheep from the 'near' side of the circuit [i.e., Maze Hairpin, Three Tree Corner, Statue Hairpin] over to The Lake Stretch, and back again for each successive lap of a race! Furthermore, they had little time to regain their breath between races before they were rushing back and forth once more, for the organization was quite the most efficient I've ever seen in the 50-odd years in which I've followed motorcycle sport. No sooner had the tail end man from one race turned into the machine paddock than the riders for the first heat of the next race were on the starting line. A few seconds late coming to that line and a rider would be excluded from the race.

I heartily concur with those who claim that the sidecar races were nearly always both more exciting AND amusing than the solos, the passenger acrobatics being quite incredible! It must be a good many years since engines of only 350cc were used regularly in sidecar racing, although in these events they frequently put up better times than the 500s, plus the fact that the sidecar races of both capacities were often faster than the solo machines. On such an intricate course with a very loose surface this is not really surprising as a top class sidecar driver could take greater liberties on the going than could an equally proficient solo rider. This is not to say that the 'charioteers' never struck trouble, they most certainly did—not a few flipping right over—bike over sidecar—and often they charged flat out through the bushes and trees that lined the course, emerging draped with vegetation like a modern army combat unit camouflaged for war. For all that I cannot remember hearing of a really serious injury to any competitor, let alone a fatality during the five seasons in which the circuit was used.

The first meeting was held on Saturday, 21st May 1927:

Fastest lap of the day was made by F. E. Parnacott [348 AJS] in 2m 7·4s, average speed 28·2 mph.

Two further meetings were held in 1927 and the course was improved by widening several sections. The best time of the day at the second meeting was made by Gus Kuhn in 1m 56s on a 348cc Velocette when he won the Kempton Cup Race for 350s. In the Catterick Cup Race for 600cc sidecars, which was won by Gordon Norchi on his 348cc Coventry-Eagle outfit, the record lap stood to Freddie Brackpool on his 495cc Matchless at 2m 5s.

RESULTS OF THE FIRST CRYSTAL PALACE MEETING

Event 1 WHITEHALL RACE 5 laps, 175cc solo, 4 starters

Trade 1 I. P. Riddoch (174 Zenith-Blackburne) 12m 32⅕s

Private Owner 1 J. D. Broughton (172 Francis-Barnett) 12m 8⅖s
2 J. Easter (172 Francis-Barnett)

Event 2 PALL MALL RACE 5 laps, 250cc solo, 4 starters

Trade 1 F. W. Clark (246 New Imperial) 11m 31⅖s
2 C. W. Johnstone (Cotton-Blackburne)

Private Owner 1 L. H. Wilson (249 Dunelt) 11m 51⅖s
2 H. C. Jeffree (249 Dunelt)

Event 3 WESTMINSTER RACE (Trade) 5 laps
350cc solo, 11 starters

1 F. E. Parnacott (348 AJS) 11m 6s
2 S. R. Twiby (348 AJS)
3 G. W. Hole (348 Raleigh)

Event 4 WESTMINSTER RACE (Private Owner) 5 laps,
350cc solo, 11 starters

1 L. Bellamy (344 Coventry-Eagle) 11m 12s
2 F. V. Porter (348 Cotton)
3 D. Wilson (344 Coventry-Eagle)

Event 5 KINGSWAY RACE (Trade) 5 laps, 500cc solo, 12 starters

1 S. Twiby (348 AJS) 10m 58s
2 G. W. Hole (348 Raleigh)
3 J. Martin (497 Ariel)

Event 6 KINGSWAY RACE (Private Owner) 5 laps,
500cc solo, 16 starters

1 J. Twitchett (499 Dunelt) 11m 23s
2 L. Bellamy (344 Coventry-Eagle)
3 D. Wilson (344 Coventry-Eagle)

Event 7 CRYSTAL PALACE SOLO GRAND PRIX 10 laps, 15 starters

1 L. Bellamy (344 Coventry-Eagle) 22m 8s
2 G. W. Hole (348 Raleigh) 22m 21s
3 B. Bragg (346 Coventry-Eagle) 22m 39s

Event 8 SOUTH TOWER RACE (Trade) 5 laps, 600cc sidecar, 3 starters

1 P. R. Bradbrook (490 Coventry-Eagle) 11m 45·6s (only finisher).
Parker (Douglas) oiled plugs, Norchi (Coventry-Eagle) shed a chain.

Event 9 SOUTH TOWER RACE (Private Owner) 5 laps,
600cc sidecar, 5 starters

1 J. E. Chell (498 AJS) 11m 32⅖s
2 A. J. Dussek (490 Norton)
3 W. Browning (490 Norton)

Event 10 CRYSTAL PALACE SIDECAR GRAND PRIX 10 laps, 4 starters

1 G. A. Norchi (344 Coventry-Eagle) 22m 1⅖s
2 P. R. Bradbrook (490 Coventry-Eagle)
L. H. Dockerill (496 Coventry-Eagle) retired lap 1
W. Browning (490 Norton) blew up his engine on lap 4

Of the third meeting in 1927, held on 22nd September, I have no details.

At this point I think it may be of interest to mention some of the famous names in motorcycle sport who competed in these races. They came from all over the country and had achieved notable successes on Brooklands Track, in the TT and Manx GP races in the Isle of Man, in speed trials, sand racing, reliability trials, grass track racing, in hill climbs and on the dirt tracks.

I. P. Riddoch, L. P. Driscoll, W. H. Phillips, H. W. Inderwick, A. M. Levenson-Gower, R. R. Barber, F. W. Hicks, F. W. Johnstone were all 'Brooklands' men, the last two equally well known in the Isle of Man, as were Len Parker, Gus Khun and H. L. Daniell, C. S. Barrow and F. W. Clark. Triss Sharp, Lew Lancaster, Roger Frogley, Miss Fay Taylor, Les Blakeborough and Gus Khun were dirt track riders while Freddie Neil, Tommy Hall, F. W. Clark and H. W. Inderwick were equally well known in the trials world. Incidentally, in gathering information for this article I have to thank Lew Lancaster, Freddie Neil and Mr. E. T. Pink for recalling for me their experiences in the path races.

Lew tells me that he raced 348 and 498cc Cotton-Blackburnes and 348cc model KSS Velocettes of which he owned two, using these machines also to ride to work on and for runs down to the coast at weekends, the only 'mods' for racing being the removal of lighting equipment and silencers. He rode the 500 Cotton-Blackburne with sidecar in one race in 1929 when his novice passenger, leaning out on the LEFT for the first right hand turn after the start, caused the bike to lift about a foot in the air and he adds that, as the cork-lined clutch burned out shortly afterwards, it may have saved them from disaster. Lew became quite well known on the dirt tracks and with the opening of the Crystal Palace dirt track in 1928 he was much a force to be reckoned with, as well as regularly occupying any one of the first three places in the path races.

Freddie Neil tells me that although most of his motorcycling was in the major reliability trials, he also competed in speed trials at Gopsal Park and on Lowestoft promenade, as well as path racing at Crystal Palace. In many of the path races both he and his 'works' partner Tommy Hall [they both rode for the Matchless factory—Collier Bros—in Woolwich, later known as Associated Motor Cycles Ltd] rode a very unusual machine, a 348cc ohc Matchless in which the camshaft drive was at the rear of the cylinder, the cylinder head being turned through 90 degrees, with the exhaust pipe on the near side, and the carburettor on the off side. 'I well remember the fiendish crackle from the exhaust of these engines,' he tells

me, 'it was beautifully built, the only plain bearing was the small-end bush, although a weakness with this design was distortion near the exhaust port'. When tuned for 'dope' it was capable of 90 mph. Freddie cannot remember being beaten for first place into the first corner after the start except by 'arrangement' with his team mate, Tommy Hall, and with this achieved, one stood a very good chance of maintaining one's lead to the finish. 'That ohc Matchless certainly had terrific acceleration'.

Eddie Pink [proprietor of motor cycle agents E. T. Pink (Harrow) Ltd] raced a P & M, very unusual! As far as I can gather it was the only time one of this marque was ridden in the races; however, he tells me he thoroughly enjoyed the races. He rode the 499cc model and finished second to A. H. Willmott [490 HRD] in the Private Owners' heat of the Nottingham Cup Race over three laps in 6m 39s in the third meeting in 1927.

You will note that the word 'Hilarity' is contained in the title of this write-

up. I suppose in the later races of the 1933–34 period a point on the lake stretch marked on the map of the circuit in the programme as 'Fuller's Dip' would have little significance for any 'new' spectator. However, there was hilarity indeed for the scratchers of the 1920s.

Its origin came about in the third heat of the CP Solo Championship for *The Motor Cycle* trophy during the second meeting on 7th August 1927. W. W. Fuller, riding his 346 Coventry-Eagle, suffered a bad attack of brake failure as he entered the lake stretch, descended the slipway at a most improbable speed—and shot into the lake! A witness later told me that there was a most impressive cloud of steam as the hot engine became very suddenly water-cooled, and poor Fuller about-faced and, with a few powerful strokes, swam to the bank—a most unusual apparition with crash hat and goggles remaining in place.

I later heard a rumour that Fuller's enthusiastic 12-year-old younger brother, acting as mechanic, had lib-

A brush past the bushes in true CP path racing style *circa* 1929. Note the slightly more purposeful attitude adopted by the riders, plus that oh, so slightly but plainly evident sophistication about the machines. Number 18 rides a Velocette engined machine although its cycle parts are not typically 'Velo' of the period in some respects.

erally squirted oil into the machine's wheel hubs, while his 'hero racer' elder brother was having a cup of tea, and that the full effect of this unnecessary lubrication did not manifest itself until the point so named on the programme map! But, as I've said, it WAS a rumour.

I acquired my first motorcycle in March 1928 and seeing that it was possible to obtain a driving licence at 14 years of age in those days, I was truly a late starter at 19½. I had been given a ride, however, on a 1920 ABC Skootamota when I was 14. I got into a wobble, shot over the bars, broke my nose and knocked out four front teeth! I hardly need to emphasize the battle

The author seated on his Zenith-JAP outside the Imperial Hotel, Great Yarmouth, June 1930. At this period the dummy belt rim front brake assembly had been replaced by a decidedly more effective drum with internal expanding brake shoes.

The Zenith is featured elsewhere in this book, being the somewhat eccentric 'star' of Mr Ashenden's Social Workshop.

Jock West with the 500cc Hartley Ariel. A paddock scene at Brands Hatch Grass Track races 1937.

I had for the next five years with my horse-age parents [bless 'em!] to ride a motorcycle after a start as disastrous as that.

Ah! my first motorcycle—a 1924 Zenith with its 344cc pukka racing JAP engine [of 1926 vintage], wide ratio Sturmey Archer gearbox having a long land operating lever direct on the box, an incredibly long wheelbase, a 'dummy belt rim' front brake that was almost useless, 6in drum rear brake being a little more effective, gas lights and 3in tyres on 26in rims. All this representing the ingredients of my first machine, it could hardly have been more unsuitable for a complete novice than one of the unwieldy big twins of the day. Its previous owner was H. W. Inderwick [already mentioned] who had ridden it with considerable success in MCC road trials— London-Exeter, London-Land's End, London-Edinburgh, etc., although I still wonder how I survived the three years I rode it without sustaining serious injury, or even worse! However, this CP Path Racing had really 'got' me, being taken to one of the 1927 meetings on the pillion of a pal's Douglas. By the time I'd got the Zenith I was a 1920s 'Ton-Up Kid'!! I turned the already dropped handlebars down still further, set my footrests further back, took the spiral baffles out of the 'carbjector' silencers [which cost my hard-up parents 50/-] and continually rode flat out in every gear—a very anti-social young horror indeed.

So it was that I entered one of the CP meetings in 1929; I was by then a member of the West Kent MC. I cannot remember the title of the race I rode in but by that time they'd dropped the 'Trade' and 'Private Owner' distinction and substituted 'A' and 'B' classes. Thinking back on my own performance there should have been a class 'D' with myself as the only entrant.

How I survived as far as Rockhills Bend before I came unstuck I cannot imagine. I was probably so scared that I rode very slowly indeed. The bike slewed right round on its right footrest and I ended up on my back, three most attractive girls surveying the prang with obvious amusement—little bitches! A gloomy figure in a long raincoat with cloth cap and a fag-end

stuck on his lip glared at me with obvious disgust.

I heaved the Zenith up, ran-and-bumped it into action and wobbled on, thinking to myself, 'I must not do THAT again', but of course I did, in EXACTLY the same spot! This time the little bitches held onto each other and simply collapsed, while the lugubrious figure in the raincoat said, 'I've gotta camp bed at 'ome, mate, yer can 'ave it fer five bob!'—swine!

I suppose by this time I'd been lapped by most of the entry and while fighting furious wobbles down the stand stretch, I was passed by a bloke with the most enormous backside I've ever seen on a motorcycle, the outstanding bum encased in a skin-tight pair of brown leather breeches. The rider was lying flat along his tank [I can imagine no racing circuit where such an attitude could be more unnecessary!] and when he was about ten yards ahead of me the breeches split—right down the centre seam—and he was wearing NO UNDERPANTS!

I've wondered since just how many other riders may have retired from a motorcycle race because they were too weak from laughter to retain control for another yard? I was nearly helpless and coasted into the machine paddock quite speechless, my mechanic thinking I'd frightened myself into a state of hysteria.

A large proportion of the 16,000-odd spectators witnessed this peculiar spectacle, and were literally rolling on the ground. However, I imagine the rider must have become aware of a cold draught by the time he got to Maze Hairpin, as he sat bolt upright in the saddle from there to the finish! Not one word of reference was made to this vulgar episode in the motorcycle press, which would seem to suggest that journalism then possibly retained a higher standard of decorum than is evident in this day and age.

I have written little about the performances of the machines in the under 175cc class. Being so very light and easily handled, they put up speeds that compared very favourably with the larger capacity classes. The Francis-Barnetts, Bakers, Coventry-Eagles, Zeniths, were powered in nearly every case by the very hot 172cc 'Brooklands' Villiers two stroke engine, and running on alcohol fuel these little motors gained most of the successes in the class. They emitted a most exciting exhaust note, an exception being the SOS machine with its water cooled Villiers motor, ridden by H. Lester. The result of the first heat of the race for under 175cc solos on 3rd November 1928 was:

1 Triss Sharpe [172 Baker]
2 H. Lester [172 SOS]
3 L. O. Bellamy [172 Coventry-Eagle]
Winner's time: 6m 16s
This was the fastest time put up by

a 175cc machine for the 1928 season and although there was no race for 250cc machines at this meeting, in the course of the whole series of these races the 250s took a minor place, the most consistently successful rider in the class being F. W. Clarke with his New Imperial.

L. O. Bellamy, riding 344 and 346cc Coventry-Eagle-JAPs won *The Motor Cycle* trophy in 1927 and 1928 and was the most outstanding solo rider. It can be said that the Coventry-Eagle reigned supreme in the majority of races, G. A. Norchi with 344 and 498cc sidecar outfits being almost unbeatable.

Nineteen twenty-nine saw the end of these races under the management of London Motor Sports and as far as I can gather the course was considered to be in such bad condition at the end of this season that it was beyond redemption. However, I have the results for the opening meeting on 16th March 1929:

Westminster Cup Race (solos under 175 cc, 3 miles)

1 J. W. Forbes (172 Baker)
2 R. S. Deller (172 Baker)
Winner's time 6m 42s

Maidstone Cup Race (solos from 175 to 350cc, 5 miles)

1 K. Dixon (346 Coventry-Eagle)
Winner's time 10m 19s.
No other finishers.

Coventry Cup Race (sidecars up to 600cc, 3 miles)

1 R. V. Newman (495 Matchless)
2 A. J. Dussek (583 Norton)
Winner's time 6m 7s

Birmingham Cup Race (solos 351 to 500cc, 10 miles)

1 R. R. Barber (495 Matchless)
2 T. F. Hall (495 Matchless)
3 R. Exell (499 P & M)
Winner's time 20m 34s

Dussek Cup Race (solos not over 500cc, 5 miles)

1 H. L. Daniell (490 Norton)
2 T. F. Hall (495 Matchless)
3 R. R. Barber (495 Matchless)
Winner's time 10m 18⅛s

Coventry Cup Race (sidecars up to 600cc, 3 miles, Grade 'B')

1 C. P. Hayward (490 Norton)
2 L. R. Courtney (493 Sunbeam)
Winner's time 6m 25⅗s

Newmarket Cup Race (sidecars unlimited, 5 miles)

1 P. V. Newman (495 Matchless)
2 F. H. Brackpool (495 Matchless)
Winner's time 10m 16⅗s

There was an evening meeting on 20th June in 1929, held in perfect weather conditions with almost as many spectators as for the usual Saturday afternoon meetings. The course was as loose and bumpy as ever, although highly suitable for dirt track riders in particular, with that most efficient 'cinder-shifter' Triss Sharpe winning the 250cc 3 mile race on a little 172 Zenith-Villiers and finishing second to Reg Barber's very hot 347 ohc Matchless [Sharp on this occasion riding a Calthorpe running on Discol] in the Grade 'A' ten mile race for 350s. Barber's time was 20m 47s, the race described in 'The Motor Cycle' of 27th June as a truly terrific scrap in which both riders lapped nearly all the rest of the field.

A one-legged man who was later to become a force to be reckoned with in sidecar racing won the Grade 'B' 3 mile race for 600 sidecars. This was the 'boss' of Taylor-Matterson Ltd of Balham, H. R. Taylor, on this occasion piloting a 498cc Coventry-Eagle outfit, his time: 6m 39·2s.

There was another heart-stopping tear-up in the ten mile Grade 'A' race for 500s, between Harold Daniell on a Norton fitted with the latest frame and tank, and Tommy Hall on his 495 Matchless. Daniell did not appear to be quite at home on this new Norton, and Tommy won after they had re-passed each other constantly, his time being 19m 58·6s.

The very last race on the circuit under the management of London Motor Sports was for the Crystal Palace Solo Championship on 22nd August 1929.

Harold Daniell won 'The Motor Cycle' cup, and in doing so twice broke the lap record, the first time from a standing start with a time of 1m 53·6s, and then with the light fading rapidly [it was a very dull and overcast afternoon], he turned his second lap in 1m 50·6s, NEARLY 33 mph! 'The Motor Cycle' report states that there was nothing wild or hectic about Daniell's riding, in fact he gave little impression of going at exceptional speed. The previous lap record had stood to the credit of Gus Kuhn on his Calthorpe and he had held it for the past twelve months at 1m 54s. At this time Gus was probably at the top of his road racing form.

The rider who came second to Daniell in this five mile race was E. C. [Eddie] Cornwell on a 348cc Cotton-Blackburne. 'The Motor Cycle' commented that Eddie was '... particularly noted for his fast and safe riding and rode consistently well throughout the meeting'.

Organized by the Streatham MCC, this meeting was the first to be held at Crystal Palace after a gap of some three and a half years. In dull conditions and with a bitterly cold wind blowing over the course, riders are seen cornering in a variety of styles while competing for the G. M. Cook Cup, 28th October 1933.

This I find not in the least surprising for in later days on the Kent grass tracks—Brands Hatch, Layham's Farm, Ashford and Barham, Eddie Cornwell on that Cotton was damn

nigh unbeatable! I knew him personally and he gave me a Blackburne racing cam one day just after the outbreak of the last war. Eddie was then manager of the Pavilion at Brands Hatch, and his famous Cotton stood in a place of honour on a stand at the end of the room. This cam produces most satisfying urge from the 348cc Blackburne engine in my 1924 Henley machine right now!

C. J. Geary, riding a 348cc AJS,

came third to Daniell and Cornwell in this 5-lap 'Motor Cycle Cup' race, the winner's time being 9m 24·2s.

I wonder how it came about at this meeting that in the race of two laps for machines up to 175cc [won by R. S. Deller on a 172 Baker in 4m 32·6s] the second man [J. M. West] was riding a 246cc OK Supreme? Jock West, of course, became a topline road racer in later years, winning two Ulster Grands Prix and finishing second in the 1939

Senior TT on the supercharged BMW. He also excelled on the grass tracks riding the Hartley-Ariels. This meeting seemed to forecast the end of the previous supremacy of the Coventry-Eagle-JAPs in both solo and sidecar racing, for in this last meeting of 1929 we see in the 5-lap race for 600 sidecars that Freddie Brackpool won on his 495 Matchless in 6m 32·4s, with two men who were to rise to great heights as high-speed 'charioteers', namely C. P.

Haywood [490 Norton], who finished second, and in the 3-lap Grade 'B' race, C. W. Sewell won in 6m 32·4s on a 348cc Velocette outfit.

Two of the well-known dirt-track riders of those days were Roger Frogley and Miss Fay Taylor, who both rode the dirt-track Rudge machines. Now I am pretty sure that a match race between these two took place on the Crystal Palace Path Circuit at one meeting, but I have been unable to

discover which year, let alone which meeting. From the few details I have unearthed however, it would appear that Fay rode a road-racing Rudge, and Roger a TT Replica Scott. Furthermore it would seem that Fay did not only win: 'Easily' (as they say of a 'walk-over' race at Henley Regatta) but that Roger fell off—TWICE! The tall and attractive Fay was certainly quite some dirt-track rider (among other notable feats she held the track

Before the hilarity passed from Crystal Palace racing activity, according to the writer. At the October 1933 meeting again, with L. A. Lloyd cornering his Norton outfit while his passenger hangs on and keeps the sidecar wheel down in true grass track fashion. Note the Norton's braced forks, being a typical feature associated with many racing sidecar machines of the period.

record in Sydney, Australia!) and from this 'Match Race' with Frogley it could be suggested that she would not have finished so very low down had she ever ridden in the Isle of Man TT!

And so we endure a gap of 3½ years before we are to be entertained once more by racing on this fascinating little circuit. The first meeting organized by the Streatham MCC was held on Saturday, 28th October 1933, the course having been 'tightened up' with some tarring on the most badly cut up sections, although it did not take the sliding sidecar outfits long to tear it up again. The meeting was held in foul weather, bitterly cold, and towards the end teeming rain. However, this did not deter as large a crowd of spectators as ever before, and they stayed to the end!

Speeds differed little from the previous meetings of 1927–29, so to give listed results could appear tedious. At this meeting a parade of riders was led by that great breaker of TT lap records (and of engines!) Jimmy Simpson on an immaculate Norton combination—and he wore a lounge suit! Harold Daniell (Nortons) was as supreme as ever, but was hotly challenged in most races by a grass track star, Johnny

Gilbert on a 348cc KTT Velocette. Jock West riding the incredibly quick 1926 500 Ariel tuned by my old friend, the late Laurence Hartley, won his heat in one race. TT riders of the future, Les Higgins and Tommy Wood, were well to the fore on their Velocettes. (T. L. Wood won the 1951 lightweight TT on a Guzzi.) In the 250 race Syd Goddard, a well-known name at Brooklands, turned out on one of the interesting Excelsior 'Mechanical Marvels'—a single cylinder 4-valve 250 with two carburettors; Sid Gleave won the 1933 lightweight TT on one of these machines. Apart from Wilf Graham's model, few Matchlesses were seen in the sidecar races, while the Nortons of H. R. Taylor, C. W. Sewell and A. H. Horton (the latter on one of the special 596cc OHC models) reigned supreme. Jack Surtees (father of John Surtees later to become both 500cc world motorcycle racing champion, and Formula I, world car racing champion) became one of the very top line grass track and short circuit sidecar exponents, finishing second to Sewell (Norton) driving a 496cc Excelsior-JAP outfit at this meeting. Karl Pugh, famous in the trials world, won a heat on a 499 Ariel, as did H. J. Addie on the 'Ulster' Rudge he rode to work on every day and later became a leading star, particularly on the Kent grass tracks.

Another was S. H. ('Jummer') Blacklocks, who rode a very hot Cotton-Python 500 (the 'Python' engine was an Ulster Rudge engine) to great effect at Brands Hatch in later years.

The three Streatham MCC organ-

ized meetings held in 1934 all maintained the same high attendance figures.

Over the 14 meetings held on the path circuit, 25 different makes of machine appeared, every one 'Made in England'! No doubt a bit of competition from overseas would have added greatly to the interest, as would the odd British machine in present-day racing, surely!

There were some interesting 'Specials' and 'Bitzas' in the 250cc races in 1927–29. For example, there was J. Twitchett's 'Gasolene Hare'—a very much modified Francis-Burnett with home-made link steering on the OEC-Duplex principle. It was very fast on corners, this oddity usually being chased furiously by J. D. Welch's similar Francis-Barnett christened 'The Paraffin Hound'.

C. W. Sewell drove an SS100 Brough Superior 1000cc V-twin fully equipped with touring sidecar and lights in a few races, and won one heat with it. Two other big twins raced were 990cc sv Matchlesses, but they could not keep the 350cc outfits in sight!

About 50 different riders competed, with entries and teams from 19 motorcycle clubs. Oh! Happy days indeed. Alas! The course eventually became so badly cut up, that it was considered finished, the June meeting in 1934 being the last of them.

A pukka hard-surface circuit of just under 2 miles to the lap was first used in 1936 and I saw one meeting on it. Exciting! Yes, but the informal element had gone and I was aware of no 'Hilarity'!

RIDING AN EMC IN THE 1949 ISDT

One man to have had first-hand competitive experience of the EMC was ED STOTT who here recalls his valiant efforts in the 1949 International Six Days Trial and some of his earlier motorcycling experiences.

Unfortunately no pictures appear to exist of Ed Stott in action on the EMC during the 1949 International and therefore it has been necessary to include a general selection of photographs of riders and machines that participated in the event. Thanks to Clifford Clegg of Blackburn who rode a BSA Bantam competition model in the classic series and who won a 'Gold' for losing no marks throughout the six days of very tough going, certain interesting pictures have been made available.

Commenting on the Trial, Mr Clegg states 'My outstanding memories are those of the interesting performance of the Hungarian Csepel two-strokes. Riding all week in their company I was impressed with the way in which even the

little 98cc machines could "see off" the British 125cc BSA Bantams on road work although they were over geared and under tyred for the rough stuff. It must have been a hard ride for the riders in consequence.'

I, Ed Stott, was lucky as a youngster. I had a number of friends a bit older than myself who all had motorcycles so I was able to absorb the whole atmosphere of motorcycling while I was still at school. This may sound odd today, when boys and girls only 7 or 8 years old or less ride regularly in sporting events, but in the 1920s there was no such thing as a Youth Division of the ACU nor today's high pressure promotion of the sport. Also, money

was not all that plentiful and you were a very fortunate lad if you had an indulgent Dad with enough cash to buy you a pedal cycle, let alone a motorcycle.

So I was lucky—my first ride happened when I was about 11 years old, when a friend with a 1923 350 Douglas suddenly said, 'About time you learned to ride. Get on.' The Douglas had a side valve engine and was a two speed belt drive model, with a clutch but no kick-starter, dummy belt rim brakes, and a 'coffee grinder' gear change on

ISDT 1949, Wales: Ed Stott seen at the Thursday afternoon's check after retiring with a broken frame on the EMC. The check at Llawnt was manned by members of the Wood Green MCC.

A veritable hive of those fascinating little 98cc Csepels seen here at the Weigh In at Llandrindod prior to the start of the '49 ISDT. In the foreground is M. Hajdu's model on which he won a Bronze Medal.

Interesting folk to the rear are George Rowley (white jacket). Harold Tozer is standing at Rowley's left shoulder.

At this period Rowley, famous AJS trials and road racing star of the pre-war scene was in retirement while Tozer as a works BSA entered driver of sidecar outfits was a Gold Medal winner in this 1949 event.

the top tube. The place where this happened was a large field near Hendon, bordering the Midland Railway main line to St Pancras [actually it had just become the LMS Railway under the 1923 grouping]. The site is now hidden, or obliterated [according to your point of view] under the Five Ways junction of the M1 motorway.

I sat on the bike, put it in gear, lifted the valve-lifter and was given a businesslike push off. It had to be paddled or pushed and was a very easy starter. Away I went, gaining speed, then changed gear as I had seen its owner do, and opened the throttle lever. To my surprise the engine coughed and faltered—unknown to me the petrol tap was 'off' and it was running on what petrol existed in the carburettor's float chamber. I worked the lever frantically when suddenly, very suddenly, the engine picked up and the Douglas accelerated, but by this time, what with looking down at the engine and operating the throttle, I was no longer circuiting the field but had

veered towards the middle. I found myself heading rapidly for the stout wooden supports of a large advertisement hoarding for Halls Distemper which flanked the railway. I hit the wooden beams a resounding 'thwack' and went down in a tangle of arms, legs and Douglas amongst the timber.

Fortunately there was no damage to the little Douglas nor injury to Ed Stott and on the principle that, after a prang, a pilot is immediately sent up again, I was picked up, put on the bike, the petrol was turned on and away I went, completing several laps of the field successfully and now enjoying the experience immensely.

Later in my riding career, when I fell off in trials, I think that very first fall was valuable, because consciously or unconsciously, I had learned that one could fall off and not come to any harm. Certainly the idea of falling off a bike never bothered me, and if it did happen, I took avoiding action instinctively.

A year or so after that first incident I acquired my first bike, a 1924 147cc two stroke Francis-Barnett, again 2 speeds and belt drive, but this one had a kick-starter. The first owner was a girl in Cricklewood, and actually my brother bought it and used it a bit, with me making some financial contribution to him. Later I bought the machine from him on an interest-free gradual payments basis, using pocket money and whatever I could earn on odd jobs outside school hours. I used to pedal around the area on Saturdays,

pasting up bills for the local cinema and so on. By the time my 14th birthday came along, the bike was mine and I obtained my first driving licence and enjoyed the freedom of the road. I used to ride the Fanny to school at Muswell Hill quite often, where I had the privilege of keeping it in the master's cycle shed!

I remember there was one other boy at school who had a motorcycle, a lad named Rodger who owned a 250 round-tank BSA, and I have often wondered since if this was the same Bernard Rodger who later made Paramount cars at Slough.

Riding my own bike soon made me some new motorcycling friends. One of these, Don Steele, also had a Francis-Barnett, a 172cc super-sports job with 3 speeds and chain drive. We rode together for many years and are still close friends. By 1931 I had got my second bike, a 1926 350 sv Enfield, and Don had changed his Barnett for a 1929 350 ohv Calthorpe, and with these bikes we joined the West Middlesex Amateur MCC and we are both still members today. We were, in fact, introduced to the club and the sporting life by another local lad, Tommy Gatrell, who had first a 172 Coventry-Eagle and then a 596 Scott Flyer, which he later changed for a 350 ohv Levis, this being a more suitable machine for his trials riding work.

We had a go at trials, grass track racing, scrambles, whatever event was on, always riding our bikes to the event

Not now clearly remembered by the author why he decided to ride the EMC rather than his trusty B32 (350cc) BSA, an example of which is shown here in a 1948 BSA sales brochure.
(acknowledgement Lewis and Sons (Weybridge) Limited)

and home again afterwards. Trailers or vans for transporting the bike were unheard of then and we couldn't have afforded them anyway. We also went to Brooklands, Crystal Palace and Donington Park when it opened, to see the racing. One of the first short 'road' circuits was at Syston Park near Grantham, where spectators could get very close to the riders as they flashed past, because with relatively small entries and rather sparse crowds, safety precautions in those days did not involve elaborate fencing and run-off areas at bends and so on. In fact, some of the early meetings had no fencing or roping at all, except perhaps for one or two spots that appeared a bit dodgy.

Although in later years our riding became more intensive as, for example, the 1949 International Six Days Trial in Wales, I look back on those pre-1939 years as possibly the best we had. The roads were truly open with very little traffic, bikes and petrol were relatively cheap, and it is only now, looking back 40 years or more, that I truly appreciate just how much fun we got out of motorcycling then.

I have been riding more or less continuously ever since, and I am still riding now. I don't care for the many restrictions we now have to put up with, I don't like the crowds of idiots who now clutter the roads, many of whom only know which is the front of the car because the seats face that way, but motorcycling is still good fun, possibly the best sport in the world.

The International Six Days Trial in 1949 was held in Wales, organized by the ACU, and many British trials riders eagerly took the opportunity to ride in such an event, using their normal trials machines but suitably modified. The regulations did not require lights to be fitted, the infamous ISDT night run had been omitted, and this made it easier to compete on a trials bike which rarely, if ever, would have any form of lighting equipment attached.

I entered originally on my 350 BSA, a B32 model which I had already

In the days when a trials bike looked as a trials bike should be, one can almost hear the bark from the exhaust of famous pre and post war trials ace F. M. (Freddie) Rist's 500cc BSA. Freddie is shown here ready to 'attack' the Aberpedwar section during the course of the 1949 International Six Days Trial. Note the tommy bar 'system' for quick release of the BSA's rear wheel also the plunger type spring heel. Swinging arm spring frames came in 1953. (acknowledgement Motor Cycle Weekly)

Without helmets and all the absurd paraphernalia that exists in trials competition today, Matchless riders R. W. M. Tamplin (124) and A. W. Burnard (125) press on through a watersplash at Abergweeyn. One wonders where EMC mounted Ed Stott was at this moment'.
(acknowledgement Motor Cycle Weekly)

ridden in the Scottish Six Days Trial but was obliged to retire with a sprained wrist after falling off on a rutted moorland track. Other events included two Nationals, the 'Beggars' Roost' and the 'Clayton'. It was a very good trials bike and I was looking forward to the International, but I cannot now—after 30 years—remember how it came about that I swapped from the BSA to the EMC. Living in North London, I knew EMC designer and manufacturer Joe Ehrlich quite well; he was, in fact, a member of the West Middlesex Amateur Club, which was also mine, and another member, named Stapleton, had ridden a 350 EMC in some of our local trials.

It was this bike that I was to ride in Wales, the arrangement being that the entry would remain as a 'private' one, and Joe would supply the bike and help to prepare it. In fact, preparation proved a bit of a headache; I had a full-time job and so would normally do any work on my bike in the evenings and/or weekends. However, on most evenings the EMC works were shut and Joe had gone home, so the work got done only at weekends, and this did not really allow sufficient time.

The engine of this works bike had port timing which gave it lots of low-speed plonk, aided by a comparatively small carburettor, and this engine was changed for one which Joe had been working on for a long time. I told him I required good acceleration all the way up the range; maximum speed was not as important as the ability to accelerate as quickly as possible on the sort of twisty going which would be the ISDT course. I can remember he spent some time measuring the ports of all the cylinder castings in the store, finally selecting one on which he did a lot of hand work on the ports with files and a grinding wheel. He then built up the complete power unit fitted with a GP carburettor and when put on the dynamometer it produced 19 bhp with a power graph giving a straight line from zero to maximum revs of 5000 or so. When I finally had the EMC on the road it certainly did have superb acceleration, although rather nullified by the wide ratios of the competition Burman gearbox, but as it had very good brakes—both hubs were conical alloy castings, like the racing Velocettes and Nortons of the period—and the handling was good, I felt it was going to be quite usable in Wales.

We managed to save quite a bit of weight by substituting a forged alloy frame backbone for the iron part which was standard. It was, of course, a rigid frame job, with the engine and gearbox sitting in duplex tubes bolted to the backbone under the steering head and the saddle. We also found a 2-gallon fuel tank which was fitted and Joe made up a very neat attachment to hold 4 spark plugs, situated under this tank.

The worrying thing about the preparation was that I did not have the opportunity to spend as much time as I would have liked working on the machine, consequently many small items which I wished to attend to did not, in fact, receive such attention. In the last week before the Trial, I arrived at the factory one evening and was told that the original wide-ratio gearbox had been changed for one with normal ratios. As I had not been able to check on the condition of the original box, it was something of a relief to know a new one had been fitted. Later, as events will show, I came to realize that this confidence was misplaced.

I rode the bike to Llandrindod on the Friday before the event, and the run down was really the first time I had been able to assess properly the EMC's performance. It was very, very noisy, and very thirsty too, and I recall that more than 4 gallons of fuel were required for the 170 miles or so; I arrived wondering if I should make the required 90 miles between petrol stops in the Trial. In fact, I did, and it seemed to be a characteristic of the GP carburettor that, on a steady

throttle opening, a lot of fuel was used, but on give-and-take going, using throttle for acceleration, then brakes, then throttle again, it was much more economical.

On the Saturday I went out to the Eppynt road racing circuit, which was to be used for the final speed test of the Trial, and did some practice laps. The EMC was not all that fast, top whack was just over 70, and I got well and truly blown off by some small European two strokes (Jawas or Csepels, I think), but the handling and brakes were very good and belting round Eppynt was a very agreeable way of spending a Saturday afternoon.

In the Trial, riders started in pairs. I was No. 210, and 209 was Jack Booker on a Royal Enfield Bullet. However, he was in the Enfield works team and on the fast schedule, so after the first check each day he gradually drew ahead, and for most of the time I was riding on my own—except for overtaking some of the riders ahead on smaller bikes.

I still have the route cards and these show the first two or three checks on the Monday to be on reasonable going.

It is described by numbers, for example—1 being 'good', while 4 was 'not good—*mauvaise—cattive—schrecklich*'. Even so, the first few miles showed up one serious fault—the EMC's Dowty front forks deflated. They used air for suspension, with a small amount of oil for lubrication of the bushes, and obviously the seals were leaking. This was a result of not being able to check them properly; indeed they were flat when I first saw the bike but seemed OK when pumped up. However, as soon as they were given some real work to do, the air disappeared and they went down on full bump, solid.

The problem was partially solved by coupling up the connection of the air-bottle (mostly used to inflate a new inner tube after fitting), but only partially. A squirt from the bottle would certainly pump them up, but as it was difficult to regulate the amount of air released—the legs then went right up on full extension, almost solid, in fact. As the pressure went down, the forks gave a tolerable action for a few miles, after which they would go right down again and the trail would alter, making navigation a bit tricky; so what with that and the hammering my wrists were taking, things were not going very well. However, I pressed on and, as I recall, managed to keep on time up to lunch.

In the afternoon, clutch trouble began to manifest itself. There was increasing free movement at the handlebar lever and, of course, gearchanging became difficult. I snatched a few moments after one check to adjust the lever on the gearbox, with no better result. Finally, the clutch would not free at all and I was stuck in third gear, causing me on one or two hills to get off and run alongside, which was a bit tiring and undignified. The climax to this trouble came as I was hammering down a nice long straight when attempting to make up lost time. There was a loud unmechanical noise, the engine screamed momentarily, then the back wheel locked, but freed itself following a loud graunching sound.

Inspection showed that the primary chain had broken, so I had to dismantle the chaincase. This was a substantial alloy affair, with the outer cover held by about twelve or so 3/16in screws. Once this was off, the reason for the clutch bother was also revealed as two of the spring-retaining nuts had unscrewed themselves, allowing the plates to open up sideways rather like an oyster, with one of the nuts finally coming right off and catching up in the chain. I repaired the chain, and screwed up the clutch springs, which was a bit of a job, as the nuts required a bifurcated screwdriver which I did not have. Compressing the springs and trying to turn the nuts at the same time with an ordinary screwdriver which was too wide to fit the slot in the nut is a job I would not have minded doing in a quiet, well-equipped workshop, but with the bike lying on its side on a minor Welsh road, with precious minutes of the time schedule ticking away, is apt to make one's patience wear thin.

Repairs completed, I set off to make up some time—at least I now had four gears all in use and a clutch that worked. However, very shortly I found myself going into a downhill left-hand bend, on a surface best described as ball bearings, which continued on a down and round course. It was useless to use the brakes as the bicycle was banked over on 2 inches of loose gravel, and I eventually hit the right-hand bank. I was somewhat winded, and the right-hand handlebar was bent down into a good short circuit racing position, suitable for Cadwell but not for the International Six Days Trial.

It is extraordinary how one can do things in moments of stress which would be virtually impossible in normal circumstances. A few yards down the hill was a stout gate. I stuck the left-hand bar in between the gate and its post, gave a good heave on the bent bar, and brought it back almost to its original position. Later on, when we tried to straighten it further using a 3ft tube for leverage, it proved very difficult, yet I had managed it without any extra help.

Cracking on again, I reached the next check 58 minutes behind my schedule, which meant that I was in the Trial by 2 minutes only (one can be up to 60 minutes late, more than that and one is automatically excluded). Although I finished the day without further trouble, indeed I even reduced my time deficit by a few minutes, I was a trifle sick about what had happened and about losing the chance of an award.

The next morning, in the 15 minutes allowed for tuning before the start, I once more had the outer chaincase off, equalized the springs on the clutch, and wired the nuts so they could not work loose again. Incidentally, this had been done on the original gearbox, but when the unit was changed, wiring the nuts was overlooked: another penalty of not being able to check off every item. Things went fairly well on the second and third days and I managed to keep on time at most checks except on two occasions when I suffered an oiled plug, always in a tight check. The loss of marks no

'Gwernoc on the Tuesday'. L. Sheaf (81) on a pre-war, watercooled, two-stroke 250cc SOS, caught in the act of changing gear (downwards) and applying an ample amount of pressure to the machine's front brake lever. Halting some rapid motion follows R. V. Holoway on a 499cc BSA sidecar outfit.
(acknowledgement Motor Cycle Weekly)

Gold medal winner Clifford Clegg 'thumbs up' as he leaves the Pont Amman check on his BSA Competition model Bantam. Note cigarette, quite a traditional way of things in the days of real trials!

longer mattered as I was not going to get anything but a finisher's award anyway, but it was a point of honour to keep on time, and not just potter along. The second day's route included the Roman road to Pont Amman and the infamous 'camouflaged gulley'. On what looked like a nice smooth grassy road where one could get into third and open up there was this terrific ditch, camouflaged by natural colour and part hidden by grass, which was very deep indeed. At the next check all the runners were telling stories of how they took off and how far they jumped and I can remember very clearly being so far forward and up in the air that my face was quite close to the Trial numberplate on the front forks. I read '210' quite clearly but upside down if you can understand! I was, of course, still using the air-bottle on the forks, so that hazards such as this were a bit larger than life.

On the third day I lost more time when, going up a steep mountain track with cross gulleys, I stood on the footrests for one of them and, as the bike crossed it, there was a loud noise and the back wheel locked. What had happened was that as I hit the gulley the footrests had been forced downwards against the serrations which located them on the frame and the left-hand rest had pressed the rear brake pedal on hard. The rests were held in position by a long threaded rod through the frame, and the left-hand nut had been forced off, leaving the thread stripped. I had a spare nut and fitted this, getting it onto some good threads by omitting the washers. The result was not very confidence-making and I had to remember, from then on, not to stand up on the rests as I would normally do without thinking when crossing gulleys and the like.

However, the bike was still a runner and I see from the time card for the fourth day that I was on time at the first two checks, even though the second one was the notorious Bidno

The somewhat hectic business of check cards being handed one way or the other particularly when one is on a tight time schedule. The situation is apparent here as Civil Service Motoring Association member S. G. M. Fitzgerald (347cc AJS) gets things over in quick time! Fitzgerald went on to win a Gold medal losing not a mark throughout the whole Trial.

Arrow indicates section where Ed Stott experienced frame breakage on the EMC during the fourth day of the ISDT.

Writing his report of the Trial on completion of the third day's activities, 'Motor Cycling's' staffman Cyril Quantrill had commented 'Quite the noisiest machine in the Trial is E. B. Stott's 346cc EMC two-stroke. Stott who had a clean sheet, lost a lot of time repairing a broken primary chain at Tregaron, but regained most of it in the Mountain crossing'.

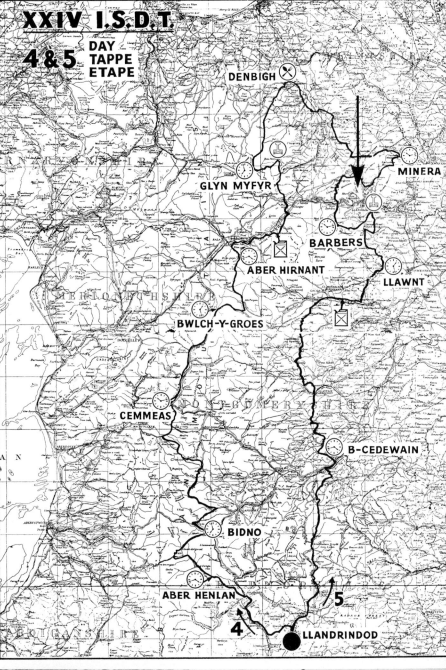

XXIV I.S.D.T.
4 & 5 DAY TAPPE ETAPE

DENBIGH
MINERA
GLYN MYFYR
BARBERS
ABER HIRNANT
LLAWNT
BWLCH-Y-GROES
CEMMEAS
B-CEDEWAIN
BIDNO
ABER HENLAN
5
4
LLANDRINDOD

section, with lots of No. 4 going, very *cattive* over the mountain, not to say *schrecklich* even. The third check, to Cemmeas, was all No. 2 type going and I was taking it easy, doing 65 or so, along a nice smooth tarmac road when there was a loud bang and the back wheel locked, and stayed locked even when I grabbed the clutch. Investigation revealed that the primary chain had lost most of its rollers, one of these breaking it, with one end of the chain lodging itself behind the clutch and against the back of the chaincase, which had cracked. To free it meant loosening the three studs behind the engine sprocket which held the inner chaincase, not an easy job as the one spanner I did not have was a big one for the sprocket nut. At least I had had plenty of practice getting out the screws which held the outer case.

By the time I got going again I was 54 minutes behind schedule and while this was not in itself important what did matter was that I was not 'tail-end Charlie', the last on the road and a long way back, so that most of the gate marshals had locked up and gone, thinking that all the participants in the Trial had gone through their particular gate. There were plenty of gates between me and the lunch check at Denbigh, as the 65 miles included Bwlch-y-groes and the Hirnant Pass, and I think I had both to open and close every gate on that route. For such operations, with a solo motorcycle, this demands a good reliable tickover, to save a continued kick-starting procedure after every gate. I had to adjust the throttle stop to give this, which meant that I lost a great deal of engine braking when the throttle was shut.

Good old Pont Amman check again. Clifford Clegg explains that as an Auto Cycle Union (N.W. Centre) member 'I handed my camera to the N.W.C. team of marshals "stationed" at Pont Amman'. Mr Clegg goes on to say that 'as a result photographic variety was somewhat limited'. Limited or not, the picture is interesting and shows Clifford Clegg (left) in cap and goggles, while the tall fellow in riding gear is the famous J. V. Brittain, who rode a 125cc James and 'clean' to the end, so winning a Gold medal. Later Johnny Brittain, son of the famous trials rider of mostly pre-war days, Vic, excelled as a works rider on a variety of Royal Enfield machines.

Later to become a Scrambles rider of considerable repute, a youthful Graham Beamish is pictured here in the 1949 ISDT having his route card stamped at the Pont Amman check. After a clean record on the first and third days, with twenty marks lost on the second, the Beamish/BSA Bantam combination retired alas on the fourth day.

However, I managed to make up a bit of time. The card states that I left the lunch check only 14 minutes behind. I had had to wait there the statutory 30 minutes and how I needed them and the food and drink provided!

A few miles later between Minera and Barbers on a bit more of best No. 4 *mauvaise route* I dropped the EMC while going up a slippery slope on the far side of a watersplash, and wrote off the clutch lever. While I was fitting a spare, a chatty Welsh farmhand came along to watch the fun and, after inspecting the bicycle (in some detail), he remarked conversationally, 'Do you know your frame's broke, boyo?' 'Oh yes,' I replied, 'It's made like that,' more to get rid of him than anything else. 'Maybe,' he said, 'But it looks proper broken to me, it does', and looking where his finger was pointing I had to admit he was right. On either side of the two bolts which held the flattened front down tubes to the head forging, the tube was cracked, clearly and cleanly, in fact a glint of bright metal showed in one gap, distinct against the enamel. I looked at the damage for some time then completed the job of fitting the new clutch lever, got on the bicycle and rode slowly over some very rough tracks to the next check at Llawnt.

Here I was amongst friends, members of the Wood Green Club and

others from the South Midland Centre who were running the check, and they were somewhat upset when I declined to give them my time card. Riding along, I had decided that broken chains, lost clutch spring nuts, bent handlebars and whiskered plugs I could cope with, but to ride a motorcycle on which the frame is held together virtually by the head-steady made from a piece of 18-gauge steel plate is dodgy enough on smooth roads, but not quite 'on' if you have to throw it round the Welsh mountains at 'international' speeds.

Naturally, when I reached Llandrindod and broke the news to Joe Ehrlich he shared my disappointment, but looking back I believe I was right. A rider in a manufacturer's or national team has a duty to finish if he can, but a private runner has some freedom of choice, and what he has to decide is whether his neck is worth the glory of finishing or not. Ignorance is bliss, and I may well have been cracking along for some time with the frame broken, but once discovered the option was 'press on or retire' and I decided on the latter.

The two following days I made myself useful helping some of the other runners, and also assisting Geoff Murdoch, who was dispensing petrol for Esso, to get his runners filled up. Then I rode back to London and retrieved the BSA from Twyford Abbey Road where I had left it before the Trial. I remember the Beesa had developed a flat tyre and I drove home pumping it up at intervals, having had enough of roadside repairs.

It was very disappointing—the previous year I had taken a 3T Triumph

out to Italy for the ISDT at San Remo and had been forced to retire with lubrication problems on the second day, so I had entertained high hopes of a better ride this time, on home ground and with some international experience to guide me. As things turned out, 1949 was not a difficult year, the weather was fine during the event and a good proportion of the private owners won awards. Among them was my friend Tom Mooney, on a 500 BSA identical to mine, who got a 'gold' quite easily on a bike which gave him no trouble, so it was not unreasonable to assume that, given a trouble-free ride, I could have got some sort of award on the EMC. Certainly there was no problem to maintain the schedule when the bicycle was going, for it went well, handled well and had good brakes. I was lucky in that I had no punctures amongst my other bothers, as the wheels were not quickly detachable.

I did gain something and that was some more experience, and I learned that good preparation for an event like the International needs adequate time. Given this time for testing, the troubles with the forks and the clutch could have been sorted out beforehand and even the chain trouble dealt with as well. The situation in the latter case was that the terrific acceleration possible put much more strain on the transmission than normal. Had we known this, possibly a cush-drive hub in the rear wheel could have been fitted.

It was a pity that another opportunity to see what the EMC in a fully prepared condition could do in an International never came along.

WHERE ARE YOU NOW?

A distant vee-twin rumble and the occasional glimpse of its awesome owner
were enough to convince DENNIS HOWARD that this was a motorcycle
worth getting to know.

I think it was the late Wilfred Pickles who once piloted a radio programme called *Where Are You Now*, in which the genial Yorkshireman managed to link up long-lost friends, reunite far-flung members of families and so on, and pushing in a familiar tune or so to assist the process along.

Now I readily accept that people are certainly more important than things and yet, in a moment of weakness, I could yield to the latter and ask any present-day Pickles type, who knows a thing or two about the whereabouts of old motorcycles, for example, to link me up with one Brough Superior sidecar outfit of a very special kind, last seen 1960 or thereabouts. If there were a possibility of a familiar tune, then let it be the rumble of that Brough's mighty—yet gentle for all that—JAP vee-twin engine . . . .

Now I never owned this Brough Superior nor ever considered that at any time I might be its owner, rather was I but a totally contented viewer of its comings and goings, with two or three glorious occasions thrown in when I actually viewed it at rest. Whether or not it may be the current custom to view a device of one's delight as a source of inspiration to better one's own motorcycle projects, I know not, but that Brough sidecar job served as a veritable tonic to me when things were getting at a low point in the garage, its appearances (usually along the A5) having me racing back to my bench determined that my own machines should have that engineering quality about them.

If my memory serves me well, the 'first sightings' of the BS were in 1946, its owner in the employ of Handley Page Limited, Radlett Division, the Brough Superior outfit taking him there every morning of what must have been his jolly life and returning him to his—would it be?—North London home in the evening. (On the last point of location I was never quite sure.) Taking a more modern day Holmesian line, I would have settled for the Brough's owner being either a toolmaker or advanced fitter in connection with Sir Frederick's aeroplanes, such was the beauty of the device in its finish and fitting of parts rather than any overworked creation. Anyway, in the 1940s there existed the splendid situation of motorcycles regularly ridden along the straight and around every corner, the day of the concours approach being many years ahead.

I will suggest in defence of any good soul who, it is hoped, might come forward to correct me, that the Brough was basically a mid nineteen-twenties SS80 model, being the 1000cc side valve job, its JAP engine looking just a little dated even by 1946 standards of appreciation, with its fir cone shaped valve caps a-top the cylinders. From the stout-hearted, tractor quality Sturmey Archer gearbox rose the familiar adjustable for any position nickel-plated gear lever', suitably long in order to permit gear changes to be made by steady hand or experienced footwork. To add a sporting touch, the owner had neatly drilled this lever along its length, the holes decreasing in diameter along their way to its tapering end.

The BS was most certainly fitted with Castle pattern front forks being of immensely strong design and working on the bottom link principle, and not dissimilar to those items that Harley Davidson machines wore for many years.

Where I have referred to the gear change lever drilled to add a sporting touch, incidentally, perhaps I should quickly add that the whole presentation of the Brough outfit was very sporting in concept and I am quite sure that this approach by its owner had me well and truly hooked—to use a modern expression.

The petrol tank was pure period

Brough Superior, a glorious flat nickel-plated affair of pear-drop section when viewed from the side, its sensuous curves willing any true admirer to place a caressing hand upon it. However, this would be an action one might refrain from putting into execution and leave solely for the pleasure of the eye! Again, the typically Brough handlebars with that special housing about the steering head end of things, but shortened so neatly as to continue the sporting flavour. Even if the inverted control levers had gone, beautifully made and fitted items of presumably aircraft quality aluminium took their place. Likewise the mudguards, where the most skilful clipping process had been performed on blades of aluminium, and no bright finish here from countless applications of one of any dozen brands of metal polish. Rather was it a case of that very special dull appearance brought on, no doubt, by clever use of wire wool and 'wet and dry' to give that serious engineering look—good stuff, yet sadly not well appreciated to this day, other than by a chosen few.

Remembered well is the generous sweep of the Brough Superior's exhaust pipes, dull nickel-plated, and so perfectly in keeping with the machine's countless other splendid parts. He who might accept the offer of a pound for any badly fitted bracket or second quality nut and bolt so spotted would have come away no richer.

Then the sidecar: surely not from George Brough's Hadyn Road works—although it just might have been—but altered much in appearance to suit its owner, the individualist working on a classic theme. I suppose I could best describe this sidecar as an ultra-sporting model based on the once very popular Launch style of things, with its tail fashioned much as the rear end of the original ERA racing car and extending some way behind the Brough's rear wheel. That feature alone did so much to make the outfit as a whole exciting to look upon and gave the immediate impression that the device was, or should have been, perfectly ex-Brooklands. Added to the body just forward of the cockpit was a diminutive aero screen, most times folded in the down position, while the sidecar wheel, sheathed on its uppermost run by yet another clipped aluminium mudguard of correct dull finish, was interesting and could not be faulted from any angle of appreciation.

Perhaps a significant clue was provided as to the origin of this sidecar for the owner had, at one time, painted a really magnificent Red Indian's head, complete with war feathers, on the forward side section of the sidecar nose. Later this was changed when an equally professional (what else?) painting of a swallow flying through a hoop replaced the Indian. However, it is just

possible that the changes were made in the reverse order.

So here was a 'once seen never to be forgotten' Brough Superior special outfit seldom driven above about 40 miles per hour during the many times I was fortunate enough to witness its movements, just the obviously effortless work provided by the meaty JAP engine, giving one a feeling of reliability and a certain solid pleasure about things. The Brough's pilot, as I remember him in the late 1940s, was a brown leather-coated figure who wore on his head a fairly loud check cap. Never did I see goggles worn, although thick black-framed glasses were always in evidence. Strangely, I never found a suitable opportunity to speak to the Brough's owner even when he stopped in Radlett village on Thursdays to purchase his usual copies of *The Motor Cycle* and *Motorcycling*. Such occasions were, however, highly suitable in permitting me to swoop down and examine this remarkable Brough Superior outfit.

By 1950 I was no longer circulating in the Hertfordshire area and had moved to London and, to a degree, thoughts of the Brough rumbling on had, by necessity, to be dismissed from my mind on other than moments of mental relaxation.

However, when travelling on the top deck of a Number 13 bus as it made its way to Golders Green in the late 50s or early 1960s, I caught sight once again of the Brough, looking just as seductive in appearance as ever as it went on its way towards Platt's Lane. As interesting was the fact that the driver was wearing a brown leather coat, a slightly less loud pattern of cloth cap and no spectacles. He was a somewhat fuller figure than the soul I remembered in the late 40s and now possessed an abundance of silvery grey hair.

Certainly it was *the* Brough and I am quite sure that its driver was 'my' original man. Unashamedly nostalgic at this moment, I call, 'Boys, where are you now?'

ROAD TESTING AN EMC

Elsewhere in this Album are to be found memories of the EMC in competition and conception. Now MIKE JACKSON lets us into the secrets of riding one of these rare machines today.

In the article 'Came but Never Conquered', on pages 58 to 63, the full working system of the EMC engine is explained.

Thanks to that well-known Puckeridge collector of more interesting two strokes, Mike Jackson, an active 1948 model EMC was offered for sampling quite recently. The word active might be stressed for out of a total of some 200 machines made available for sale in the United Kingdom during the five years of EMC manufacture, only eight or nine are known to exist here in the whole at least, while actual runners are reduced to but two or three.

Purchased as a non-runner in the late 1960s, however, by Mr Jackson, the EMC was hastily made operational in order that its owner could make a trip to the Isle of Man Manx Grand Prix races in 1973. Treated carefully on this occasion, the machine gave little trouble.

A 1948 EMC model nicely restored by its owner Mike Jackson. Two noticeable changes from the previous year's specification were the fitting of a conical front brake drum assembly instead of dual brakes of Vincent

HRD manufacture, and a throttle controlled oil pump. The latter fitment was a decided advantage over the manually adjusted hit and miss, so many pulsations to the drip Pilgrim pump formerly fitted. A clever adaptation of the Pilgrim instrument, the pump was of the 'built in' type with a mechanical plunger in which a taper valve synchronized with the throttle, varied the oil flow to the engine's big end and rear cylinder, according to the throttle openings. Originally a twin cable twist grip was fitted for the purpose, although with Mike Jackson's model a special 'junction box' is employed. The pump's control cable can be seen on the lower left part of the pump. Note the oil feed pipe to the inlet and exhaust cylinder.

Dedicated two stroke enthusiast and owner of an excellent collection of models and types, Mike Jackson is pictured here demonstrating by careful throttle position the EMC's surprisingly low tickover speed. Meanwhile, Dennis Howard prepares for a few 'getting to know you again' runs before embarking on a spot of 'serious' stuff.

Just visible on the bike's cast iron cylinder block are the smaller cooling fins set in between the larger ones. The idea was, according to Joe Ehrlich, that as the block heated up the differential cooling provided by such a system would give a corrugated bore in each cylinder thus holding oil in the low spots. Whatever—an interesting theory.

Airship weather, overcast with constant drizzle as the writer takes a spin on an EMC for the first time since 1949. Spoilt by riding regularly more up-to-date machines, the EMC was, however, a surprisingly pleasant thing to pilot with plenty of torque, good low-down pulling power and no tendency to four stroke when running lightly. Exhaust note as ever but a muted burble from the huge Sackville absorption type silencer, issuing here the 'traditional' steady blue haze. Hidden by the rider's leg is the BTH TT type racing magneto and Lucas dynamo for the 6 volt lighting system. The Schrader valve housing can just be spotted at the top of the Dowty forks. Wheel sizes, 20in front and 19in rear.

Rebuilt correctly and in line with original specification the following year for a run to the TT races, rather major engine troubles were experienced on the outward journey to Liverpool docks.

In the owner's words . . . 'The bike was cruising well when suddenly a distinct change in the EMC's going took place near Junction 13 [pure coincidence!] on the M6 motorway. Whatever the trouble that had certainly come about in the engine department, I knew that it was of a sufficiently serious nature to require my abandoning the machine, and fortunately friends of the family who lived not so far distant from the M6 were able eventually to remove it and put it under cover. I did notice, however, before leaving the EMC that a certain bulge now existed on the

A very 'different' motorcycle of British manufacture in the early post war period, the EMC was much an acquired taste. However, one might have hoped that eventually it would have proved to be a commercial success, following suitable development.

crankcase and the internal disorder had literally sprung the engine outwards. Later, when I had the opportunity to strip the engine down I was alarmed to find that the slave 'transfer' connecting rod had completely parted from the master rod at the knuckle joint. This meant that for a short time before I was able to bring the bike to a halt on the motorway very unpleasant things had occurred in the works department between the free rod and the still revolving parts until a jam of everything took place. It is often the very simplest things that are eventually found to be the cause of a major catastrophe, for in the case of the EMC, I discovered that the little steel ball which normally locates the wristpin upon which the slave connecting rod is secured to the knuckle joint had, in some amazing way, departed from its seating. In such circumstances the wristpin would have 'wound' itself out of the knuckle joint housing, thus releasing the rod from capture. It does not require a great deal of imagination to appreciate the damage so caused from that point.' Fortunately, Mike Jackson was lucky enough to obtain a spare engine and with this he has been able to make one really good unit out of the parts of two. Since that last

enforced rebuild the EMC has proved to be a very reliable mount, so much so that it is used regularly by its owner and treated in much the same way as one might do with any modern motorcycle, although perhaps there is just a slightly more sensitive approach to the bike's motion, in view of its age and the memory of matters arising at Junction 13 a few years ago.

Ridden to the 1979 TT races, the EMC was cruised at a speed of about 45 mph (3000 rpm) and returned, believe it or not, that 100 miles to the gallon of petrol, making Mike's model above all others in the road-going Ehrlich breed.

What better, in a nice part of rural Hertfordshire, than a quick gallop on FNT 194. Suddenly, all the memories return to the writer of his trip to Silverstone on a similar model for the first motorcycle race meeting held there thirty-three years ago. Anything goes, and goes well with the EMC's 18 bhp produced as the fancy takes one. Try some ups and downs on the 4 speed heavyweight Burman gearbox . . . splendid boxes these. Of the general roadholding and steering, 'good enough but don't take liberties', and the brakes are just fine in the hands of a skilled operator. In the writer's opinion the EMC was—and indeed remains—no bad machine, but it's a strange device: the very stuff that makes life interesting.

THE ONLY RISING SUN

This thought-provoking treatise on engine design by technical expert BILL FIRTH explores the 'whys and wherefores' of the unconventional Honda Gold Wing and looks at some fascinating earlier projects.

Mr Firth has been described as a 'senior' man and indeed so when one learns that motorcycles he has owned were glorious things like two-speed Scotts, camshaft Nortons and Sunbeam 500s.

Now living in Nevada, Bill Firth was at one time on the editorial staff of the journal 'The Engineer' and rode fifty miles a day into London on 'Black Bitch', being his S7 model Sunbeam, the machine on which, Mr Firth says, the front spindle did not keep the forks in line and where one braked with long, strong fingers.

The author long ago maintained that the best machine does not necessarily win in the marketplace and set himself the

task of finding out why this was so. Bill Firth then adds, 'the answer, being obvious, took all my powers to discover, for the best man wins only in a fair fight, only in free competition, only where there is, in the language of law, no prior restraint'.

Having discovered this, he is now engaged in 'defending earth's last bastion of liberty' . . . Nevada.

Mr Firth lives in a one hundred year old wooden house situated between the historic US Mint and the Governor's mansion in Carson City, enjoying here very much the new life. Readers of the old OLD MOTOR MAGAZINE will,

of course, remember the many technical articles contributed by Bill that appeared in its pages over many years.

In North America, one can hear a Japanese proper noun, *Honda,* used as a common noun generic to small, powered vehicles . . . The products of the incredibly prolific giant of the Orient includes not only all the conventional two, three and four wheeled vehicles with single cylinder, parallel twin and straight four engines, but also transverse V twins like the Guzzi, straight sixes like the Benelli and transverse fours like . . . like . . . like what?

Left The 999cc Honda 'Gold Wing' in standard form weighs 604lb. Notice the four constant velocity carburettors and two disc front brakes. The large flat cover in front of the cylinder head encloses the toothed timing belt.

Above The 1085cc 'Interstate' has a valanced front mudguard, crash bars and fitted luggage as well as protection for the rider. Above the rear end of the right-hand camshaft can be seen the fuel pump, necessary because the 5-gallon tank is under the saddle. Note the composite wheels with alloy rims and steel spokes.

The Honda Gold Wing is unlike any other machine, and even unlike its own image. What appears to be the fuel tank in fact encloses the charging system, fuel filler, toolkit, storage space and coolant header tank. *Coolant*? Yes, the engine is liquid cooled, with a thermostatically controlled electric fan. Electric *fan*? Indeed, for without a fan the coolant would boil if the machine was brought to a halt and the engine left running. Coolant, a fan, anything *else*? Well, yes, there are four constant velocity (that is, variable choke) carburettors, and a fuel pump, because the fuel is not in what looks like the tank, set above the carburettors.

How, one may well enquire, did Honda arrive at this culmination? The answer is at once apparent, by adopt-

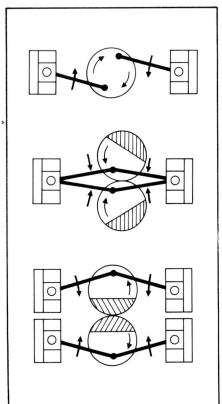

The conventional opposed twin, as built by Douglas and BMW, has a primary rocking couple about the crankshaft axis, due to the inertia of the connecting rods: even if the cylinder bores were colinear, the engine would not be perfectly balanced. (Top.)

Lanchester's twin employed three connecting rods for each piston, and since the rods to the top crank were moving in the opposite direction to those on the bottom crank, no couple was excited. The masses of the pistons were balanced by counterweights on the crankshafts. (Centre.) The geared-crankshaft Brough added to the perfect balance of the Lanchester evenly-timed power strokes, with the convenient left-right-left-right firing order that the ordinary four lacks. (Bottom.)

ing an opposed four engine. Any simple four cylinder power unit has the inconvenient left-left-right-right firing order that demands a choice between one carburettor and four, while the opposed four has the further disadvantage that direct cooling of the heads (cooling by air) is possible only with a symmetrical flow—top to bottom, or inside to outside—and thus the great advantage of air cooling on a motorcycle (where the motion of the machine affords the cooling) is abandoned.

There is, of course, good reason why the opposed four is so popular in cars and aircraft. The crankcase is very light and the crankshaft very stiff, and if high speed is not critical, a single central cam can be used to operate the valves in both cylinders. Continental aero engines exploit this configuration to the ultimate, and use the timing gear reduction also to drive the propeller. However, there is a great difference between cars and motorcycles. Cars have long ceased to use the crankcase to stiffen the frame, motorcycles—with rare exceptions such as the Sunbeam S7 and S8, with two universals in the drive shaft—do not allow the engine freedom to vibrate within the machine.

Why should the engine vibrate? This is a question readily answered by reference to one of the oldest and greatest of scientific laws, Sir Isaac Newton's conservation of momentum. Newton, we may recall, saw an apple fall off a tree and said, 'I don't believe my eyes . . .', his theory being that if one thing accelerates in one direction, something else accelerates in the opposite direction, thus, as the apple starts its downward journey, the earth must come up to meet it. After more than three centuries, no experimenter has ever created or destroyed any momentum, so we must expect that if the piston goes down, the engine will go up.

There are three approaches to this problem. The first is, to clamp the engine into the machine and hope that, as the rider is also attached to the frame, he won't notice the frame move. This is the approach typical of the British parallel twin, the enormous balance mass in the middle of the crankshaft contributing greatly to making the stress in the shaft and the load on the bearings constant, but very little to smooth out the forces on the engine mountings. To be specific, it changes an oscillating vertical force of 100 into a constant force of 50, rotating backwards.

The second approach is to provide a system where the engine can move without deranging the transmission of power to the back wheel, as in the Norton Commando. In principle, if the centre of gravity of the power unit is somewhere in the transmission, then a vertical oscillating force in the engine will produce no movement at all about a point somewhere behind the transmission.

The third approach is to arrange that when one piston goes down, something else within the engine is going up, so that the engine itself doesn't move at all.

The obvious thing to move in opposition to the piston is another piston and this has been the favoured approach from the early days (Douglas) to the present (BMW). However, even if the pistons were exactly opposed and, for example, were located in the same bore, there would still not be perfect balance. The designer usually imagines that the only moving masses are the piston and the crankshaft, working on the assumption that the connecting rod can be considered as two masses, one at the crankpin and the other at the gudgeon pin. However, this is not so, for the rod acts as if its

Late 1930s. Sensational Broughware—the Golden Dream.

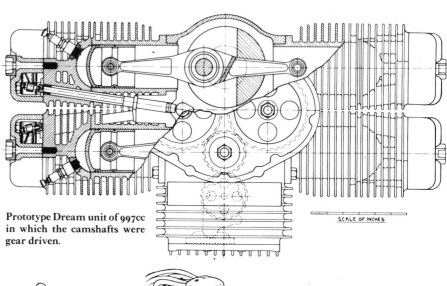

Prototype Dream unit of 997cc in which the camshafts were gear driven.

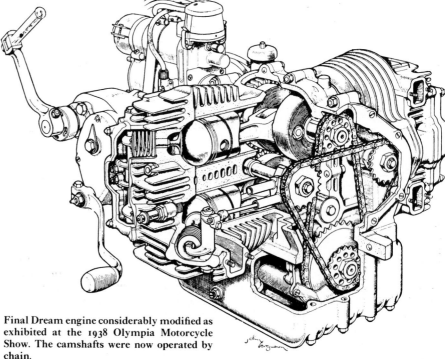

Final Dream engine considerably modified as exhibited at the 1938 Olympia Motorcycle Show. The camshafts were now operated by chain.

mass were concentrated at its centre of gravity, which is, if the rod is not counter balanced, somewhere above the crankpin. Therefore, the opposed engine will suffer a rocking couple about the crankshaft axis, due to the inertia of the rods. This couple will oscillate at engine speed and have its maxima at mid-stroke.

The greatest theoretician of the early days, if not, indeed, of any days, saw that the alternate firing twin could not be balanced, and proceeded to devise a twin that could be. F. W. Lanchester's design balanced the three different disturbances in three different ways. The primary forces were balanced by masses on the counter-rotating crankshafts, which was possible because the two pistons moved in phase. The secondary forces balanced each other out, because the two pistons were on opposite sides of the cranks. In addition, the forces generated by the connecting rods were also balanced, because each piston had rods to both of the cranks. Being a perfectionist, Lanchester used three rods to each piston, the outer two going to one crank and the inner one to the other. Not only was this engine perfectly

balanced when running at constant speed, it also exhibited no 'torque reaction' under acceleration. The Honda has the alternator rotor on a countershaft, so that the machine does not roll when the engine accelerates suddenly in a gear change. It did, however, have one disadvantage, with a firing order at intervals of 180-540-180-540. The subsequent 180-180-180 Lanchester engine was only a straight four, with primary forces balanced and the secondary forces additive.

However, the obvious improvement to the Lanchester engine was made in England. The legendary George Brough saw that if the two pistons were replaced by four, to attain even firing, then the six connecting rods

could be replaced by four in turn. Moreover, the engine would now fire left-right-left-right, and accept two carburettors, while with the cylinders one above the other, an air flow along the crankshaft axis, as in a motorcycle, was ideal for cooling.

Thus a perfectly balanced four cylinder engine without space-wasting, counter-balanced connecting rods, was built in the late 1930s to power the Brough Superior Golden Dream.

The Brough four had the perfect balance of an opposed six without the problem of cooling a centre cylinder and with immunity from 'torque reaction'. Well might it be said, 'They don't build 'em like we used to . . .'

BALANCING OUT THE FORCES

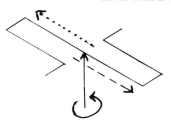

Fig 1 Crankshaft and pistons of an opposed twin at outer dead centre. The primary forces on both pistons are inward, but the forces are offset and give rise to a couple.

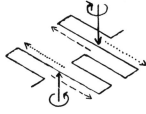

Fig 3 In an opposed four the primary couple generated by the first pair of pistons is balanced by that of the second pair of pistons.

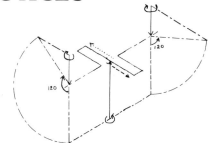

Fig 5 The centre cranks and pistons of an opposed six at outer dead centre have a primary couple vertically upward. The front pair of cranks would have a couple 120° to the left and the rear pair of cranks a couple 120° to the right. Thus the couples would balance— a couple of 100 upward would be opposed by two of 50 downward.

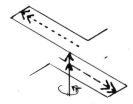

Fig 2 Crankshaft and pistons of an opposed twin at inner dead centre. The secondary forces on both pistons are inward and again give rise to a couple.

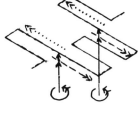

Fig 4 In an opposed four the secondary couple generated by the first pair of pistons and that generated by the second pair, add together.

The familiar engine with connecting rods between the crank and the piston exhibits two different kinds of inertia forces.

The first is the obvious kind. At top dead centre, the piston is accelerating downward, so there must be a downward force driving it, and at bottom dead centre it is accelerating upward, so there must be an upward force acting on it. This force, then changes in magnitude from maximum downward to maximum upward and back to maximum downward in one revolution, ie, at one times engine speed, so it is called a *primary* force.

However, there exists another force, due to the connecting rod being less than infinite in length. Because of the shortness of the rod, the piston has more acceleration at top dead centre than at bottom dead centre. Indeed, if the rod was as short as the crank throw there would be *no* acceleration at bottom dead centre! Thus this acceleration is downward at top dead centre

and downward at bottom dead centre. At all events we know that the average acceleration must be zero, since there is no change in velocity from one revolution to the next, so we infer that it is upward at mid-stroke. This other force, then, goes from maximum downward to maximum upward to maximum downward in half a revolution, so it is called a *secondary* force.

The secondary forces present most of the problems. Any force can be balanced out by a pair of eccentric masses rotating in opposite directions at the same speed, but rotors running at twice engine speed present a most undesirable complication.

An attractive approach to balancing the forces is by having a second piston with a motion equal but opposite to the first one. If, however, the cylinder axes are off-set, to allow the two rods to run on separate cranks, the two equal and opposite forces add up to a *couple* attempting to turn the engine about an axis at right angles to the

crankshaft and to the cylinder axes. The primary couple is in one direction at outer dead centre (*Fig 1*) and in the opposite direction at inner dead centre; the secondary couple is in the same direction at outer dead centre as at inner dead centre (*Fig 2*).

In an attempt to balance out the couples, the obvious move is to add a second pair of cranks at 180° to the first pair. This does indeed result in the primary couples being cancelled (*Fig 3*), but turning a crank through 180° turns the secondary forces through 360°; thus the secondary couples of the two crank pairs add together (*Fig 4*), showing the opposed four to be no better than the opposed twin.

The simplest engine with both primary and secondary balance is the six; turning a crank pair through 120° to the right turns the secondary couple through 240° to the right, ie, through 120° to the left, so three pairs of cranks at 120° intervals do indeed balance (*Fig 5*).

INDEX

Abbott, Ray 6, 7, 10, 11, 12, 13, 14, 15
ABC Skootamota 69
ACU Quarterly Trials 11
Addie, H. J. 74
Aermacchi (motorcycle) 26
AJS (motorcycle) 12, 17, 31, 36, 37, 64, 67, 68, 72, 81
Alexander, A. H. 10
Amulree 11
Anderson, Fergus 28
Applebee, F. A. 10, 11, 13, 14
Arbuthnot, Rear-Admiral Sir R. K. 13
Ariel (motorcycle) 17, 44, 68, 69, 70
Arms Hill 12, 13
Ashford 72
ASL (motorcycle) 12

Baker, Jesse 12
Baker (motorcycle) 71, 72
Banbury Run 65
Barber, R. R. 68, 71
Barbers 83
Barham 72
Barbook Mill 12
Barnes, F. W. 11
Barrow, C. S. 68
Bashall, W. H. 12
Bateman, F. R. 13, 14
Beamish, Graham 83
Bedford Modern School 74
Beggars Roost Trial 78
Bellamy, L. 68, 71
Benelli (motorcycle) 92
Birdlip 12
Blacklocks, Jummer 74
Blakeborough, Les 68
BMW (motorcycle) 43, 72, 93, 94
Booker, Jack 79
Brackpool, Freddie 67, 71, 72
Bradbrook, P. R. 68
Bradbury (motorcycle) 12, 13, 14
Bragg, Bill 68
Brands Hatch 65, 72, 74
Brewster, D. 18, 19
Briggs sidecars 51
Brittain, J. V. 82
Brooklands 7, 11, 13, 31, 37, 38, 43, 48, 61, 68, 77
Brough, George 12
Brough, motorcycle 12
Brough Superior 74, 84, 93, 94, 95
Browning, W. 68
BSA (motorcycle) 30, 35, 36, 75, 76, 77, 78, 81, 83
BTH magneto 88
Burman, Hans 60, 62
Burnard, A. W. 78
Butler, P. 12
Bwlch-y-Groes 82

Cadwell Park, 79
Calthorpe (motorcycle) 71, 76
Campbell, Sir Malcolm 47, 48
Campbell, Bluebirds 48
Castle forks 85
Cemmeas 82
Centaur (motorcycle) 11
Chater-Lea (motorcycle) 11
Chell, J. E. 68
Chipping Norton 14
Choisey, Raol de 64
Clark, F. W. 68, 71
Clarke, F. 13
Clayton Trial 78
Clegg, C. 75
Clyno (motorcycle) 10
CM (motorcycle) 26
Collier Bros 68
Cornwell, E. C. 71, 72
Cotton 68, 72
Cotton Blackburne 68, 71
Coulson Blackburne 30
Countisbury 12
Cook, W. E. 12
Courtney, L. R. 71
Coventry-Eagle (motorcycle) 30, 67, 68, 69, 71, 72, 76
Crystal Palace 48, 64, 65, 77
Csepel (motorcycle) 75, 79

DKW (motorcycle) 51, 61
Dancers End 39, 41
Daniell, Harold 66, 68, 71, 74
Dashwood Hill 7
Davies, Rev B. H. (Ixion) 11
Dawson, J. 10
Deemster light car 15
De Havilland Rapide 65
Deller, R. S. 71, 72
Denbigh 82
Dixon, K. 71
Donington Park 77
DOT/Bradshaw (motorcycle) 30
Douglas (motorcycle) 10, 12, 68, 70, 75, 76, 94
Doverhay 37
Dowty forks 61, 79, 88
Driscoll, L. P. 68
Drake 6
Ducati (motorcycle) 26
Dunelt (motorcycle) 68
Dusseck, A. J. 68

Easter, J. 68
Edinburgh Trial 42
Edward VII 10
Ehrlich, Joe 59, 61, 63, 78, 83, 87
EMC (motorcycle) 58, 59, 61, 62, 75, 78, 86
Enfield 12
English-Dutch International Trial 15
Eppynt Road Race circuit 79
Excelsior Manxman 26, 58
Excelsior Mechanical Marvel 74
Exell, R. 71
Essex Trial 44
Exeter Trial 42, 43

Fitzgerald, S. G. M. 81
Forbes, J. W. 71
Ford, Model T 19
Francis-Barnett (motorcycle) 68, 71, 76
French Grand Prix 14
Frogley, Roger 68, 73, 74
Fuller, W. W. 69
Fuller's Dip 69

Gasolene Hare 74
Gatrell 76
Geary, C. J. 72
Gilbert, Johnny 74
Gilera (motorcycle) 26
Gleave, Sid 74
Goddard, Syd 74
Godfrey, O. C. 10
Graham, Wilf 74
Greaves, H. 12
Gwernoc 80

Hajdu, M. 75
Hall, Tommy 68, 71
Hammett, Miss 7, 12
Handley Page 85
Hardee, Miss 7, 12
Harley Davidson (motorcycle) 22, 85
Hartley, Laurence 74
Haslam, J. 11
Haswell, J. R. 7, 9
Haynes, T. 23
Hayward, C. P. 71, 73
Heaton, Billy 12
Henley Blackburne (motorcycle) 29, 65, 72
Henley-on-Thames 13
Hicks, F. W. 68
Higgins, Les 74
Hirnant Pass 82
Hole, G. W. 68
Hollaus, Rupert 27
Holloway, R. 12
Honda (Gold Wing) 92, 93
Horton, A. H. 74
HRD (motorcycle) 69

Inderwick, H. W. 68, 70
Indian (motorcycle) 7, 14, 18, 19, 20, 22

JAP 30, 84
Jackson, Michael 86
Jarrott Cup 13

Jarrott Cup Trial 10
Jawa (motorcycle) 79
Jeffree, H. C. 68
Joad, Professor C. E. M. 65
Jones, A. S. 9
Johnston, F. W. 68
Johnstone, C. W. 68

Keppel Gate 13, 14
Kop Hill 10, 15
Kremleff 14
Kuhn, Gus 67, 68

Lancaster, Lew 68
Lanchester, F. W. 93, 95
Layhams Farm 72
Lee-Evans 7
Lester, H. 71
Leveson-Gower, A. M. 68
Levis (motorcycle) 58, 76
Llandrindod 83
London-Land's End Trial 3, 36, 37, 41, 42
Lloyd, L. A. 73
Lord, R. 10
Lorenzetti, Enrico 23
Louis, Harry 28
Lynmouth 12

Mallee, The 20
Mallory Park 65
Manx Grand Prix 66, 68, 86
Martin, J. 68
Massetti, Umberto 28
Matchless (motorcycle) 7, 11, 13, 16, 67, 68, 69, 71, 72, 74, 78
May, W. E. S. 13
Mayer, Alex 24, 25
MCC Inter Team Trials 14
MCC Tenth Anniversary Team Trial 14
MCC High Speed Trials 38
McMinnies, W. G. 11, 12
Melbourne 18, 19, 20, 21
MG Midget 36
Milan-Taranto Road Race 27
Minera 83
MM (motorcycle) 26
Mondial (motorcycle) 28
Mooney, Tom 83
Morgan, H. F. S. 12
Morgan (three wheeler) 12, 30, 33, 64
Motor Cycle, The 28, 29, 30, 33, 64
Motor Cycling 29, 85
Moto-Guzzi (motorcycle) 23, 24, 25, 26, 27, 28, 74, 92
Munro, L. C. 7
Murdoch, G. 83
MZ (motorcycle) 50, 53, 54, 56

Nap Hill 15
Neil, Freddie 68
Nesono, Signor 27
New Imperial (motorcycle) 31, 68
Newman, R. V. 71
Newsome, W. F. 11
Norchi, Gordon 67, 68, 71
Norton, J. L. 11
Norton (motorcycle) 11, 31, 33, 49, 66, 68, 71, 72, 74, 92
NSU (motorcycle) 7, 12, 27
NUT (motorcycle) 10

OK Supreme (motorcycle) 72
Olympia, Motorcycle Show 34

Paraffin Hound 74
P & M (motorcycle) 6, 7, 12, 16, 69, 71
Parilla (motorcycle) 26
Park Royal 61
Parker, H. E. P. 12, 13
Parker, L. 68
Parnacott 67, 68
Phelon, Joah 16
Phillips, W. H. 68
Pickles, Wilfred 84
Pink, E. T. 68, 69
Pont Amman 80, 82, 83
Porlock 12, 37
Porter, F. V. 68

Premier (motorcycle) 12
Puch (motorcycle) 61
Pullin, C. G. 15

Quadrant (motorcycle) 15
Quarter Bridge 13

Radlett Village 85
Raleigh (motorcycle) 68
Ramsey Hairpin 12
Redhill Flying Club 65
Rex Speed King (motorcycle) 10
Riddoch, I. P. 68
Rist, Freddie 77
Royal Enfield 79, 82
Rudge (motorcycle) 7, 13, 14, 15
Rudge Ulster model 58, 73, 74
Ruffo, Bruno 28

Sackville Silencer 88
San Remo 83
Schrader valves 88
Scofield, E. W. 11
Scott (motorcycle) 7, 12, 13, 14, 30, 31, 63, 64, 73, 76, 92
Scottish Six Days Trial 78
Sewell, C. W. 73, 74
Sharpe, Triss 68, 71
Shaw 6
Sheaf, L. 80
Sheard, T. M. 14
Shepreth Motors 65
Silverstone 65
Simpson, Jimmy 74
Six Days 6, 11
Snaefell Hill Climb 10
Sproston, A. J. 10
Stapleton 78
Steele, Don 78
Stevens, A. J. 12
Stonebridge, Brian 16
Sturmey Archer 85
Sunbeam (motorcycle) 71, 92, 94
Surtees, Jack 74
Super Onslow Special (motorcycle) 71, 92, 94
Sutteism 11
Swiss Grand Prix 28

Tamplin, R. W. M. 78
Taylor, Fay 68, 73
Taylor, H. R. 71, 74
Territorial Army 47
Territorial Camp 49
Triumph (motorcycle) 7, 9, 11, 12, 13, 15, 18, 37, 38, 39, 41, 42, 44, 46, 47, 48, 64, 83
TT Races 7, 8, 9, 10, 11, 12, 13, 18, 27, 28, 37, 46, 67, 68, 72, 74, 90
Turner, Edward 17
Twiby, S. R. 68
Twitchett, J. 68, 74
TWN (motorcycle) 61

Ulster Grand Prix 23, 72

Velocette 37, 38, 66, 67, 68, 73, 74
Vincent HRD (works) 41
Vincent HRD (Rapide model) 41, 43, 44
Vintage MCC 65

Waders 4, 5
Welch, J. D. 74
West, Jock 70, 72, 74
West Kent, MCC 30
West Middlesex Amateur MCC 78
Willmott, A. H. 69
Willoughby, V. H. 28
Wilson, D. 68
Wilson, L. H. 68
Wood Green MCC 75, 83
Wood, Tim 7, 13, 14
Wood, Tommy 74
Woodhouse, Jack 15

Zenith Blackburne (motorcycle) 68
Zenith Gradua (motorcycle) 11
Zenith JAP 29, 30, 33, 64, 69, 70, 71
Zenith Super Eight 64
Zschopau 51

ACKNOWLEDGEMENTS

The author and publishers wish to thank the following for the use of illustrations:

The Motor Cycle for pages 4, 22, 28 (lower), 44 (upper), 46, 65; A. B. Demaus for pages 6–15 (all); David Ansell for pages 16, 17, 59; Margaret Craig-Collins for pages 18–21, 22 (upper); Terry Haynes for page 23 (upper); G and Friends Studio for pages 23 (lower), 26 (all), 27 (upper); Dr Helmut Krackowizer for pages 24, 27 (lower), 28 (upper); Penny Wilde Studio for page 29; Roger Beale for pages 30, 32; Norman Sanderson for pages 34–43 (all), 45, 47, 48, 49; Peter Dobson for pages 50–57 (all), 86–91 (all); Michael Jackson for pages 60–63 (all); BBC Hulton Picture Library for pages 64, 72, 74; Eric Thompson for pages 66, 69; Guy Ashenden for pages 67, 70 (both); Ed Stott for page 75; Alan Burnard for page 76; Lewis & Sons for page 77 (upper); *Motor Cycle Weekly* for page 77 (lower), 78, 80; Clifford Clegg for pages 80–83 (all); *Motor Cycling* for pages 85, 94 (upper and lower); Honda Motor Company for pages 92, 93 (upper); Bill Firth for pages 93 (lower), 95; Ronald H. Clarke for page 94 (middle).